Rhymes of Early Jungle Folk

A Replica

of the 1922 Edition

Featuring the Poems of Mary E. Marcy

with Woodcuts by Wharton Esherick

Foreword by Laura Heemer

Edited by Paul Eisenhauer

Schiffer Publishing Ltd

4880 Lower Valley Road • Atglen, PA 19310

Published by Schiffer Publishing, Ltd.
4880 Lower Valley Road
Atglen, PA 19310
Phone: (610) 593-1777; Fax: (610) 593-2002
E-mail: Info@schifferbooks.com

Other Schiffer Books by the Author:

Wharton Esherick Studio & Collection, ISBN 978-0-7643-3449-8

Wharton Esherick and the Birth of the American Modern, Paul Eisenhauer and Lynne Farrington, editors, ISBN 978-0-7643-3788-8

Poplar Culture: The Celebration of Esherick's Tree, ISBN 978-0-7643-4208-0

Other Schiffer Books on Related Subjects:

Esherick, Maloof, and Nakashima: Homes of the Master Wood Artisans by Steven Paul Whitsitt and Tina Skinner, ISBN 978-0-7643-3202-9

Wharton Esherick's Illuminated & Illustrated Song of the Broad-Axe by Walt Whitman, ISBN 978-0-7643-3677-5; Limited Facsimile Edition ISBN 978-0-7643-3678-2

Library of Congress Control Number: 2014958489

ISBN: 978-0-7643-4937-9
Printed in China

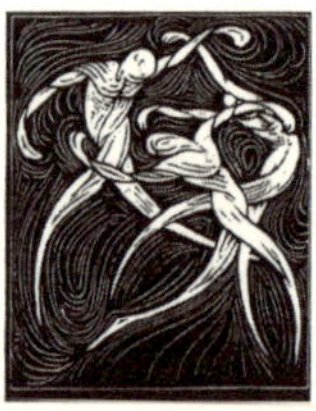

Wharton Esherick Museum
www.whartonesherickmuseum.org

Foreword

How We Did Play

Rhymes of Early Jungle Folk, originally published in 1922, was the result of a chance meeting between Wharton Esherick and Mary Marcy. In the winter of 1920, Wharton Esherick travelled with his family to Fairhope, Alabama, so that his wife Letty could study progressive education at Marietta Johnson's School for Organic Education. Wharton's experience there would revitalize his career and turn the painter into a wood sculptor. At the same time, Mary Marcy, the editor of the *International Socialist Review* (the *ISR*) was in Fairhope looking for rest and renewal. It was here that the two would meet and the idea for *Rhymes of Early Jungle Folk* was born.

Mary Edna Tobias Marcy, born May 8, 1877 in Belleville, Illinois, had a difficult childhood. Both her parents died while she was still young and Mary was forced to work to support herself through high school. Her difficult childhood led to an interest in radical politics. In 1896, she was fired from her job for wearing a button that supported the Democrat William Jennings Bryan. Clarence Darrow, a well-known attorney and civil libertarian, came to her aid, securing a job for her as an office secretary for the president of the University of Chicago. Her position provided her with free tuition which Mary took full advantage of, studying psychology, English literature, and philosophy.

In 1899, she and her husband Leslie H. Marcy moved to Kansas City, where Mary found a job as secretary to the treasurer of a large meat packing firm. In 1903, Mary joined the Socialist Party and became an active member. The recently established *International*

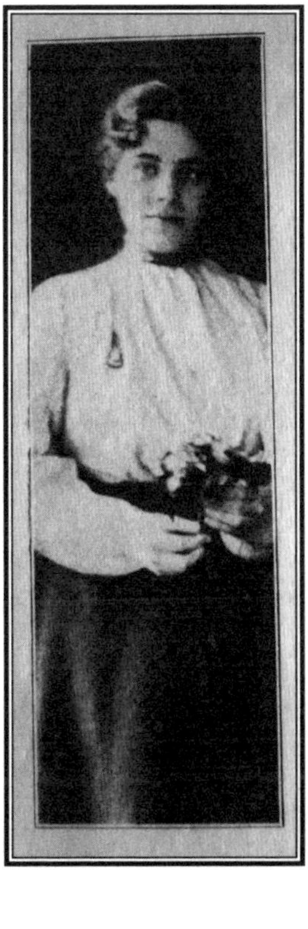

Mary Marcy; date and photographer unknown. Originally printed in *Mary E. Marcy – Memories*, 1922. Wharton Esherick Museum archives.

Socialist Review ran a series of letters penned by Mary called "Letters of a Pork Packer's Stenographer," which exposed the dangerous working conditions and poor wages of the laborers. Her letters in the *ISR* gained national exposure, and she was subpoenaed to appear before a Chicago grand jury to testify against her employers, an action that would once again cost Mary her job.

The Charles H. Kerr Publishing Company had been established in 1886 by Charles Hope Kerr to promote his Unitarian views, but as his personal interests moved from religion to Marxism, he became interested in the labor movement and the company's publications followed suit. Kerr began to publish the *International Socialist Review* in 1900. In 1911, Charles H. Kerr & Co. reported a circulation of 17,000 subscribers and an additional 32,000 copies sold over the counter per issue. In 1908, Mary returned to Chicago to work for Charles H. Kerr & Co. as an assistant editor for the *ISR*. Mary was a perfect fit for the company, and worked as the secretary, a contributing writer, and an editor for fourteen years. Several of her series of articles in the *ISR* were published as books by Kerr, and became significant publications of the Socialist movement.

With the American declaration of war against Germany on April 6, 1917, the *ISR* became a target of government suppression, including the United States Post Office Department placing them under surveillance and denying their use of the mails. Without access to its subscribers, the publication was terminated in 1918. In that same year, Mary joined the Industrial Workers of the World (IWW).

As a result of government surveillance, the Marcys' home was ransacked by the U.S. Department of Justice in a search for evidence of war resisters, and all of her papers and belongings were confiscated. Mary sank into a deep depression. Shaken by political persecution and great personal loss, she traveled to Fairhope to recover in the warm climate and seek solace in the artistic community there.

Mary befriended Wharton and Letty Esherick, and her friendship with Wharton transformed into an artistic partnership. Building on an earlier book, *Stories of the Cave People*, she began work on a children's book of verse. She wrote a series of 54 poems on evolution and prehistoric peoples, a highly controversial subject at the time. This publication would come three years before the benchmark Scopes "Monkey Trial" of 1925 that resulted in the inclusion of the teaching of evolution in public schools. Mary wrote to Wharton asking him to illustrate her book. Drawn by the excitement of the controversy and the alignment of his political beliefs, he heartily agreed.

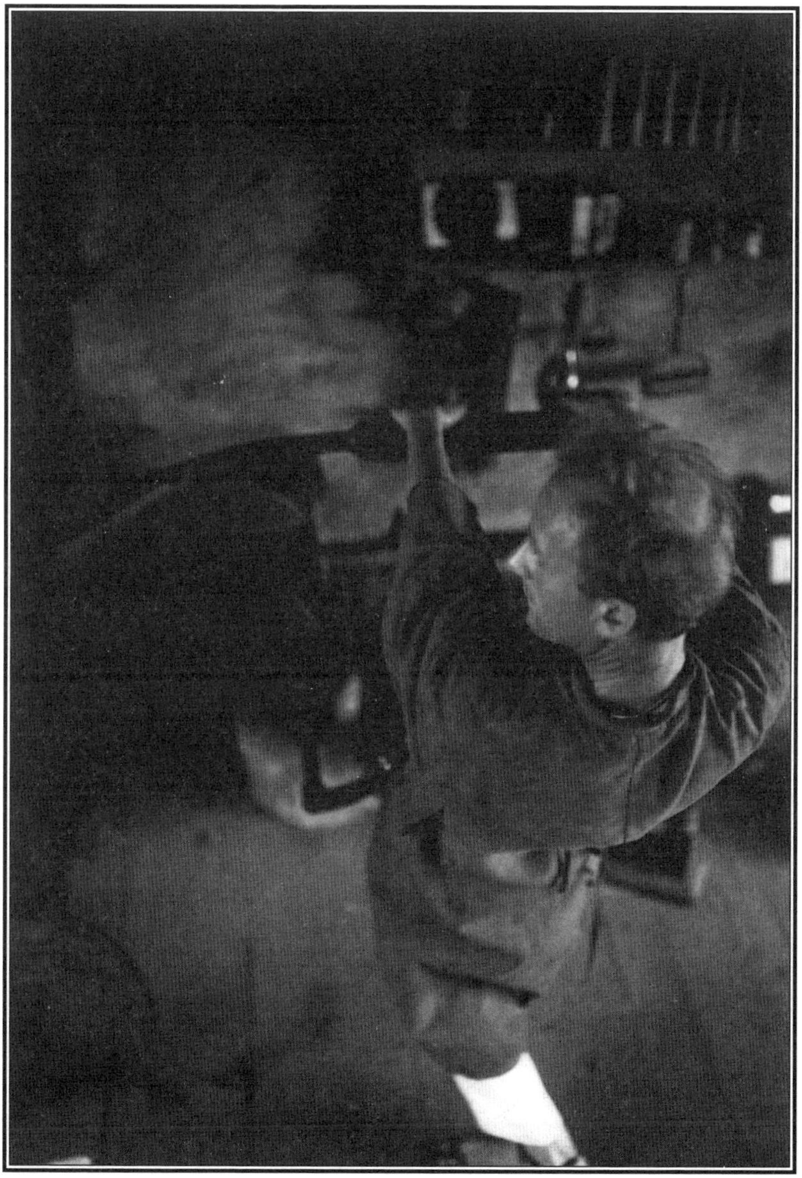

Wharton Esherick at his printing press.
Photograph by Emil Luks, c. 1930.
Wharton Esherick Museum archives.

While in Fairhope, Wharton had acquired a set of carving tools in order to carve frames for his paintings. Enjoying carving, he decided to illustrate Mary's book with woodcut prints. Mary would send a completed poem to Wharton, who would carve a corresponding woodcut and send it back. Wharton carved 100 woodblocks for *Rhymes of Early Jungle Folk*, 78 of which were used in the final publication. His woodcuts for *Rhymes* were rough and rudimentary, yet dynamic, fun, and whimsical. He enjoyed the process of carving, and in the woodcuts one can see the foundation of Wharton's voice as an artist. After *Rhymes*, Wharton would go on to carve over 300 woodcuts and illustrate several other books including The Centaur Press editions of *Song of the Broad-Axe* by Walt Whitman in 1924, and the biblical account of *The Song of Solomon* in 1927. The woodcuts led to decorative carving on furniture, toys and games for the children, and ultimately, Wharton's realization that he was a sculptor rather than a painter.

Though Mary enjoyed her work on *Rhymes*, the depression that had set in after the ransacking of her home and the disintegration of the American left after WWI continued to take its toll. In 1921, Mary and her husband mortgaged their home to provide bond money for IWW organizer William "Big Bill" Haywood, who was being held as a political prisoner. When Haywood jumped bond and escaped to Soviet Russia, Mary and her husband lost their home. Shortly after the publication of *Rhymes of Early Jungle Folk*, Mary committed suicide by poison.

Wharton was shaken by her death—their friendship had deepened over the course of their work together. For a memorial booklet, Wharton created a woodcut to commemorate his friend. Wharton said of Mary:

> Mary was a woman with a fine soul and willing to work and the socialist movement recognized and dragged her in. I wish her seed had fallen on an artistic ground instead of political, her strength of conviction, her playful philosophy would have created much, much more. But she got into this radical socialism and being true, loyal, and willing she stuck and pushed. Underneath her words in letters to me, I find crying, reaching for a flower, a butterfly, a bird to toy with. How we did play in our letters. It was business but we played together and had fun. *(Esherick notes, 1923)*

In reproducing *Rhymes of Early Jungle Folk,* the Wharton Esherick Museum wishes to honor the high regard that Wharton had for Mary. We feel that the book displays the pleasure they took in work and play, and the fun they had in working together. This authorized edition of

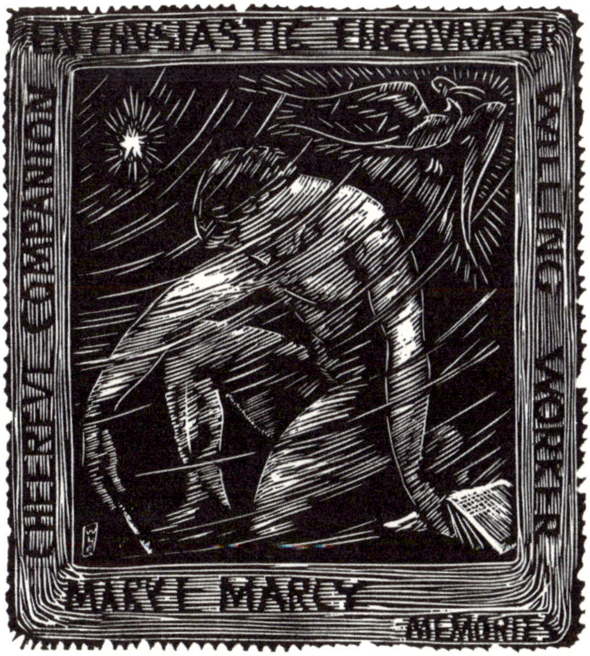

Mary E. Marcy – Memories, 1922.
Wood engraving by Wharton Esherick for the cover of *Mary E. Marcy – Memories*.
Wharton Esherick Museum archives.

Rhymes of Early Jungle Folk preserves the original layout and design, while compensating for the effects that aging and earlier technology had on the original edition.

We would like to thank the Charles H. Kerr Publishing Company for their permission to reprint *Rhymes,* as well as Pete Schiffer and the hardworking team at Schiffer Publishing for making this quality reproduction possible. We would also like to thank the David A. and Helen P. Horn Charitable Trust for their support of the preparation of this book and of the Wharton Esherick Museum's family and education programing. As always, we are grateful to the Esherick family for their unwavering cooperation and support.

Laura Heemer, Assistant Curator
Wharton Esherick Museum
Paoli, PA

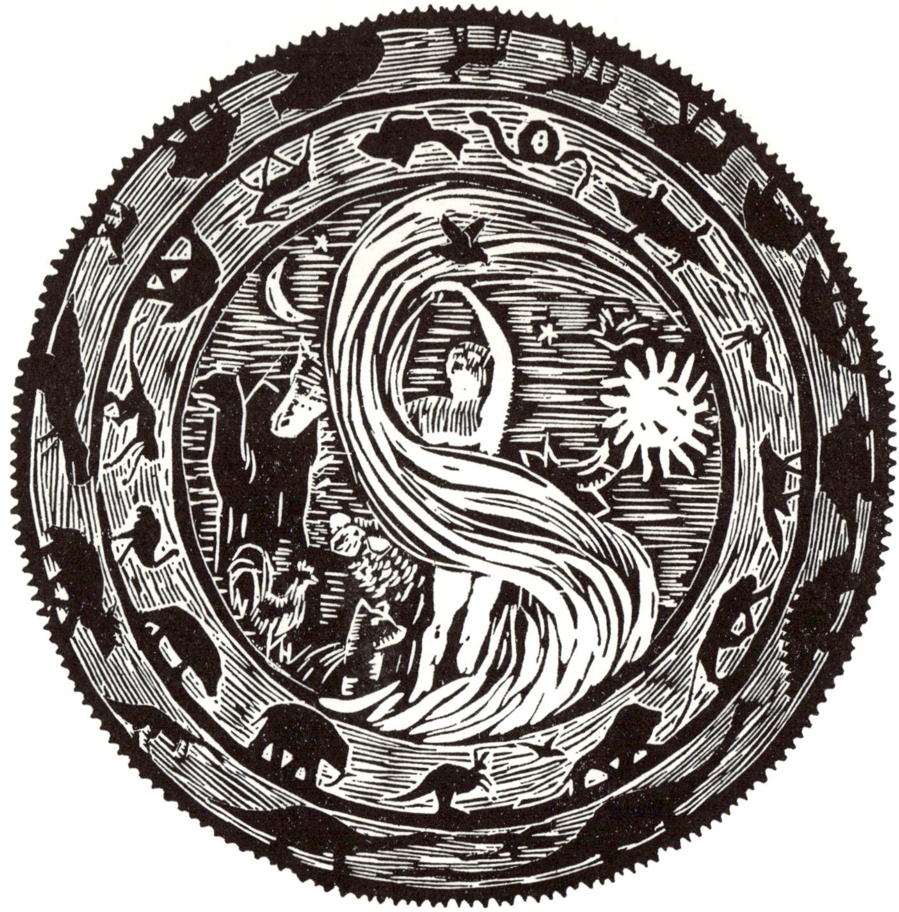

RHYMES of EARLY JUNGLE FOLK

by

MARY E. MARCY

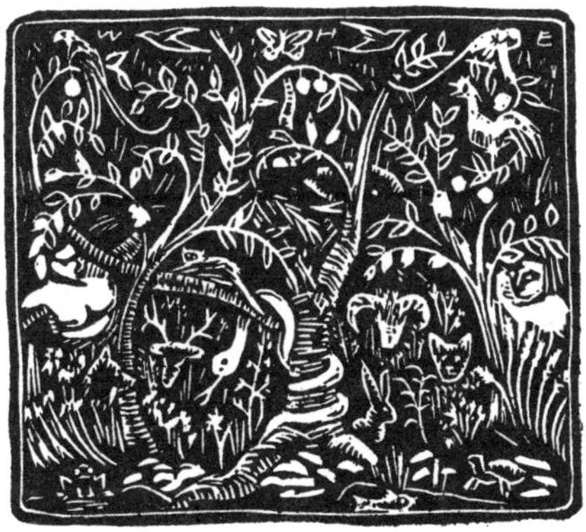

WOODCUTS by WHARTON H. ESHERICK

PUBLISHER
CHARLES H. KERR & CO. CHICAGO

Printed in the United States of America.
80

TABLE OF CONTENTS

RHYMES OF EARLY JUNGLE FOLK

ONE TIME OUR PLANET WAS A SUN

One time our planet was a sun,
That burned within the sky;
Perhaps folks watched from other worlds,
To see it whirling by.

And then its blazing surface cooled,
As every surface must,
And covered all the fire with
A hard and rocky crust.

And when the rains began to fall,
They covered it with ocean,
That tossed and foamed from pole to pole,
In manifest commotion.

A great and mighty water world!
A blazing mass inside,
Which bent the crust and lifted it
Above the water tide.

So came the first and rocky shore,
The prehistoric land,
Where now we live and love and learn,
And try to understand.

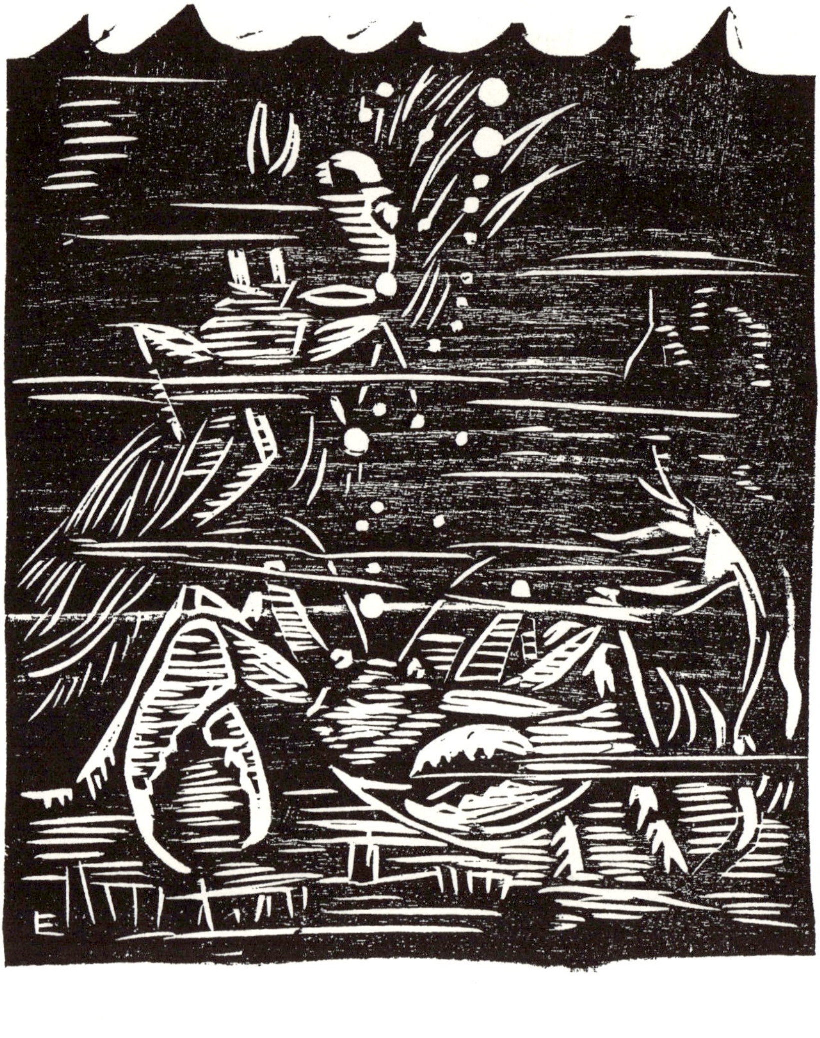

WHEN THE PLANTS CAME OUT

WHEN THE PLANTS CAME UP OUT OF THE SEA

In the Pal-e-o-zo-ic-al Age,
Say the men geologically sage,
  Scattered over the land,
  Were great oceans of sand;
'Twas a barren historical page.

For—there wasn't a bird or a bee,
A tuffit of grass, or a tree;
  There was nothing to eat;
  There was no one to meet,
For the animals lived in the sea!

There were scorpions bigger than men,
Who were kings of the water woods then;
  There were crabs hairy-footed,
  And plant-animals rooted,
Ere the days of the land folks began.

But the plants were tossed up on the shore,
And they could not get back any more,
  But they had to have drink,
  So they started to sink
In their roots on the land, and to bore;

Where they sucked up the water with ease,
And they lifted their boughs to the breeze;
  So they grew in the sun,
  And the trees were begun,
From the flora tossed up by the seas!

Thus the weeds tumbled out on the foam,
And they thrust in their roots for a home,
  Where they grew and they spread,
  In a green earthy bed,
And they made a rich surface of loam.

WHEN THE ANIMALS CAME FROM THE SEA

And some of the fish began to climb,
To wriggle, crawl, and creep,
And wallow in the swampy slime,
To hunt, and eat, and sleep.

At first they dared not venture far,
When they were safely landed;
Their home was in the water, and
They felt they might be stranded.

And here a monster dragon flew,
And spread his wings so wide,
They might have hidden half a house,
And several men beside;

And here the giant boa crawled,
On short and clumpy legs,
That looked like stumps of willow trees,
Or clumsy oaken pegs.

And weighing sixty thousand pounds,
He ate a ton of meat,
To satisfy his appetite,
When he sat down to eat.

A reptile, the di-plod-o-cus,
An hundred feet in length,
The vicious bron-to-sau-rus,
With his stupid, slimy strength;

The unappeased at-lan-to-saur,
With jaws as wide as doors,
From which the camp-to-so-rus fled,
With Mes-o-zo-ic roars!

An ocean covered all the land,
  Where now are fertile plains,
And farmers in the Central States
  Raise pigs, and cows, and grains!

And as I sit upon our porch,
  I often wish I knew,
If here the di-no-sau-rus walked,
  And pter-o-dac-tyls flew!

I wish I'd seen those reptile things,
  That crawled and wallowed then,
But I am glad I wasn't born,
  Before the Age of Men!

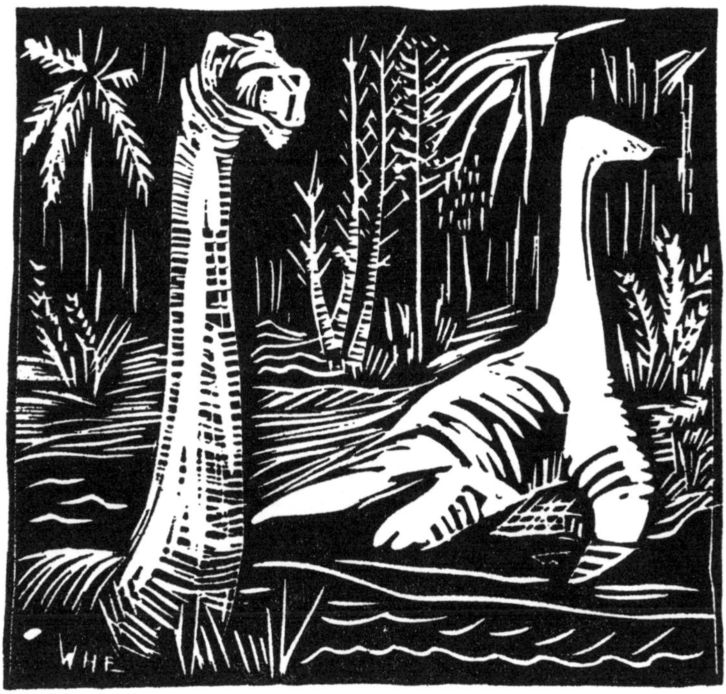

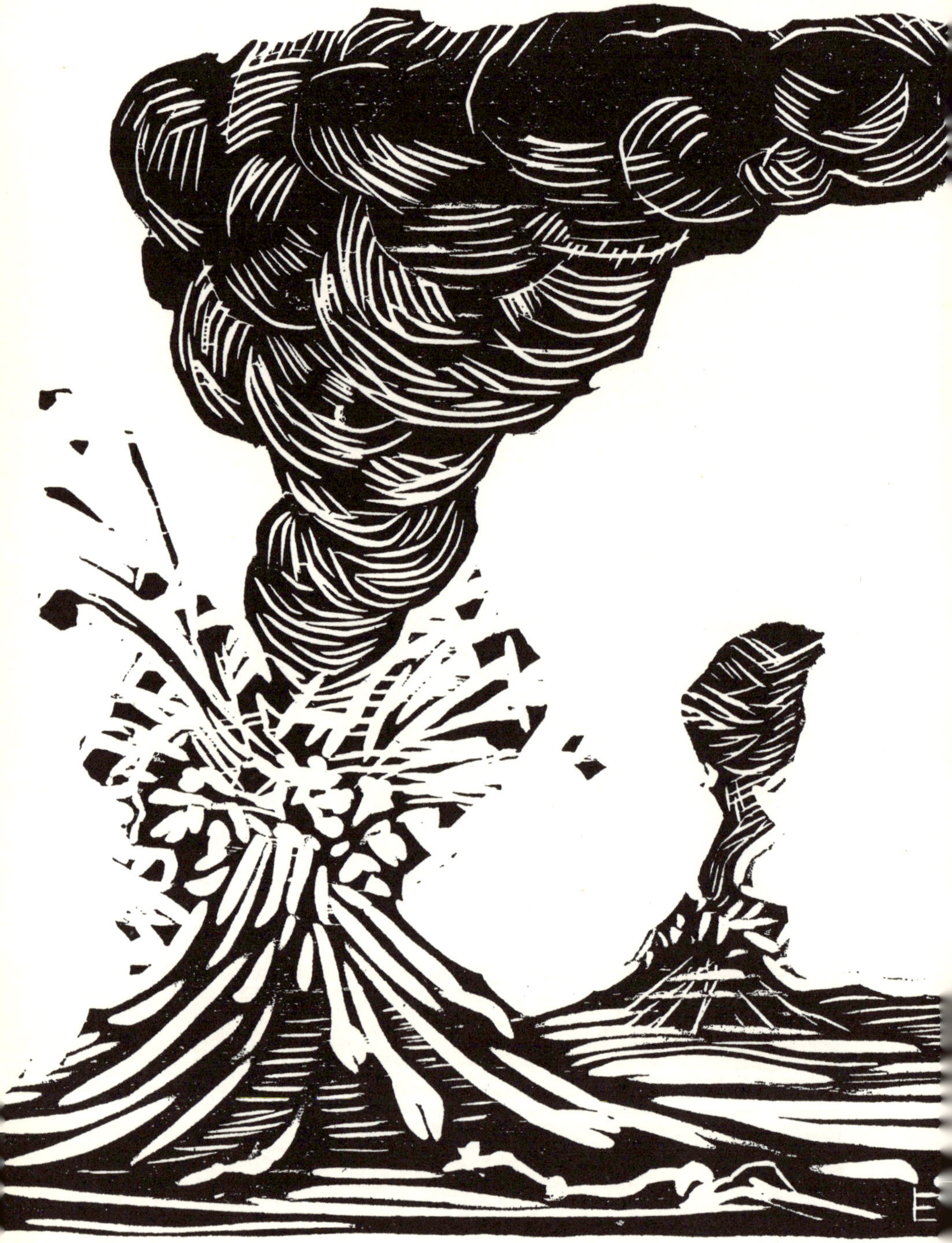

INSIDE THE EARTH

Our world is very hot inside;
  It twists and writhes and doubles,
As blazing gases rise above
  The molten lava bubbles.

Sometimes there isn't room enough
  For flaming gas expanding,
And so it pushes up the crust,
  To leave great mountains standing.

Again, the flaming gases swell,
  And roar for space, and grumble,
And shake the surface of the world,
  Where earthquakes rock and rumble.

Or else they split a mountain, and
  We see volcanoes blowing,
Like soda in a giant glass
  That foams to overflowing!

I wish that we could catch the heat,
  That thunders forth to harm us,
And pipe it to our northern lands,
  To cook for us, and warm us!

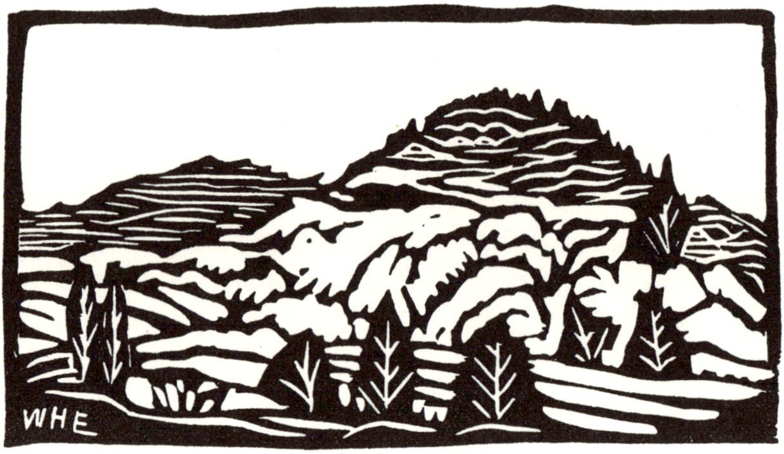

HOW COAL WAS FORMED

There were marvelous jungles that grew in the swamp,
  And tangled themselves in the marsh,
    When the land was all steaming,
    And new life was teeming,
  And never blew winds that were harsh.

The great e-qui-se-tums, the palms and the ferns,
  With stems which were thicker than trees,
    Were tough as the logs,
    And down deep in the bogs,
  Thrust their roots with the cal-a-mi-tes.

The pine tree was there, carboniferous king,
  The cy-cads, as tall as a church,
    And mammoth club mosses,
    With climbings and tosses,
  Were hardy and thick as a birch.

The horse-tails grew straight, and as high as a maple,
  And everything grew like a weed;
    A new time was sounding,
    All life was abounding,
  And groping to satisfy need.

And whenever a tree tumbled down in the mudlands,
  And shivered and wallowed and sunk,
    A dozen young shoots
    Thrust their hungry young roots,
  And started to grow on its trunk.

And so they continued for seasons and seasons,
  Till the mass was as dense as a wall,
    Trees embraced one another,
    And trampled each other,
  And the cy-cads grew sturdy and tall.

Then the mountains arose and the rivers flowed down,
  And they covered the jungles with earth;
    Caused new forests to grow,
    Over old ones below,
  In a new vegetational birth.

At last came a time when volcanic eruptions
  Poured down and extinguished the whole,
    Where the forests, in tiers,
    Buried millions of years,
  Were pressed into our wonderful coal!

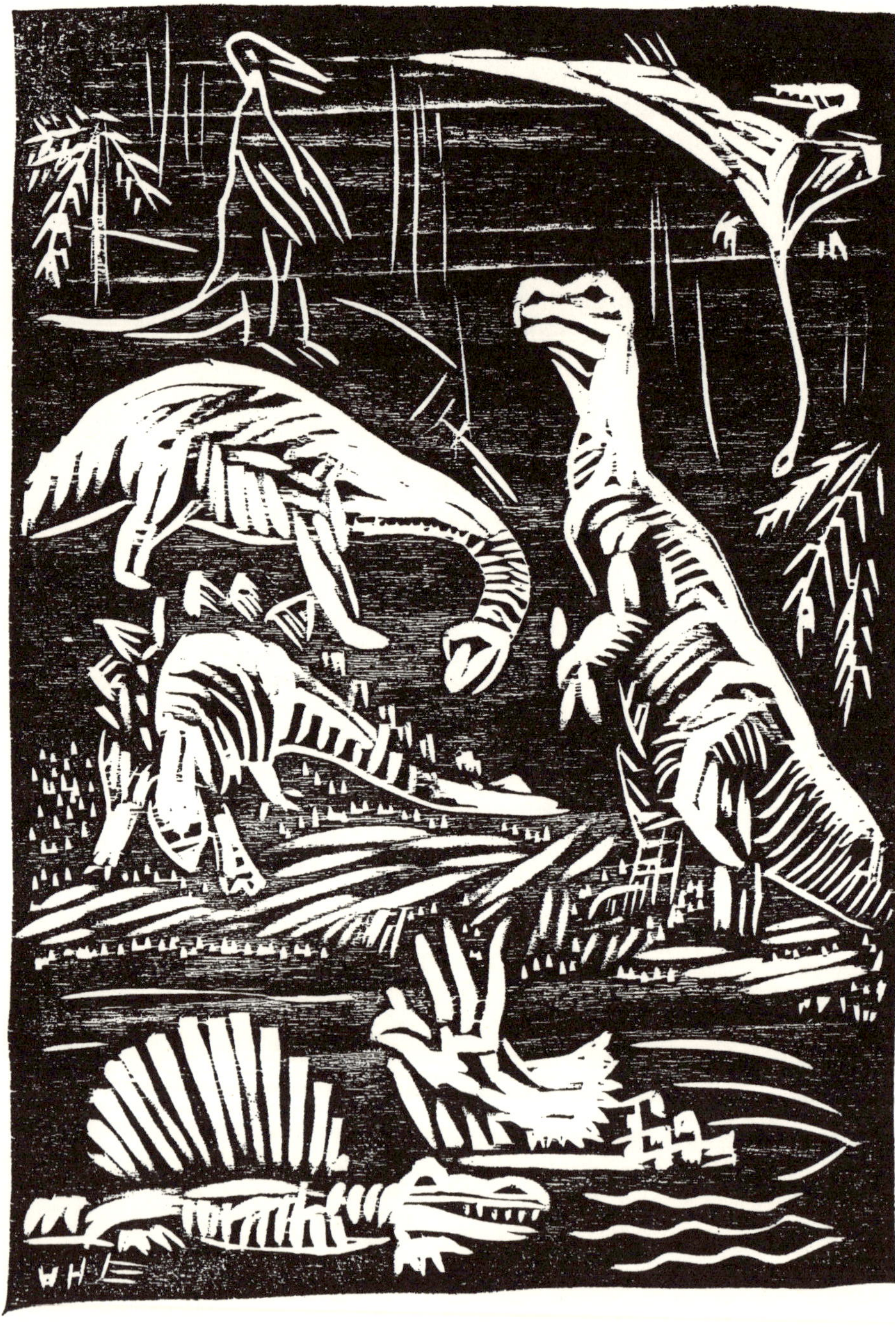

THE REPTILES

THE COLD-BLOODED ANIMALS
(of the Mesozoic Era)

There were no human beings in the Mes-o-zo-ic stage,
And we aren't sure the mammals entered here;
At least they left no fossils in the strata of that Age,
When the earth was very swampyfied and queer.

Of course the the-ri-o-mor-phus was a reptile quadruped,
And we can guess by looking at his bones,
That he might have been the cousin, very distant, it is said,
Of a mammal, but this point is still unknown.

The birds had jaws like reptiles, and they had a row of teeth,
Three claws upon the corner of each wing;
They wore a fringe of feathers on a bony tail beneath,
And there's naught to prove they ever learned to sing.

And there were mammoth mo-sa-saurs that crawled about and flopped,
The porpoise of that wet and torrid clime,
And there were massive kangaroos that ate the leaves and hopped;
I'd tell their names, if I could make them rhyme.

And tortoises, and turtles too, and snaky crocodiles,
And tra-cho-dons, ty-ran-no-saurs, and bats,*
Of the family of lizards which could skim a dozen miles,
And climb a tree as agile as the cats.

At first they all lacked cozy scales, and feathers, fur and hair;
Their blood was cold; the climate kept them warm;
They loved the steaming tropics for their slimy skins were bare,
And they sought the sunny marshes in a swarm.

*(Note: bat-lizards)

CHANGE! CHANGE! CHANGE!

The change was abrupt,
But it did interrupt
  The lazy reptilian rule;
Perhaps the earth tipped,
And its axis was slipped
  To the poles we have heard of in school.

The weather turned cold,
And the Winter grew bold;
  He reigned over most of the year,
While the reptiles, with skin
Which was naked and thin,
  Succumbed in a bleak atmosphere.

But the few that had fur,
As it chanced to occur,
  Were all dressed to exist in the snow;
The hairy and feathered,
Adapted, so weathered
  The winds, and the ice and the blow!

The Age Ce-no-zo-ic
Required the stoic,
  In order to grow and survive,
A living contraption,
With gifts of adaption,
  And the mammals began to arrive.

The beech and the hollys,
Say the wise anthropollys,
  Appeared with the ivy and gum,
And trees of new classes,
And plains with their grasses,
  And flowers where honey bees hum.

It was during this time,
That a drama sublime
  Made the earth's surface crumple and shrink,
And the mountains arose;
As geology shows,
  There were portions beginning to sink.

With a giant upheaving,
Himalayas were cleaving
  The air and the clouds and the sky,
The Alps and the Andes,
A pair of high grandees,
  Who smile on the life passing by!

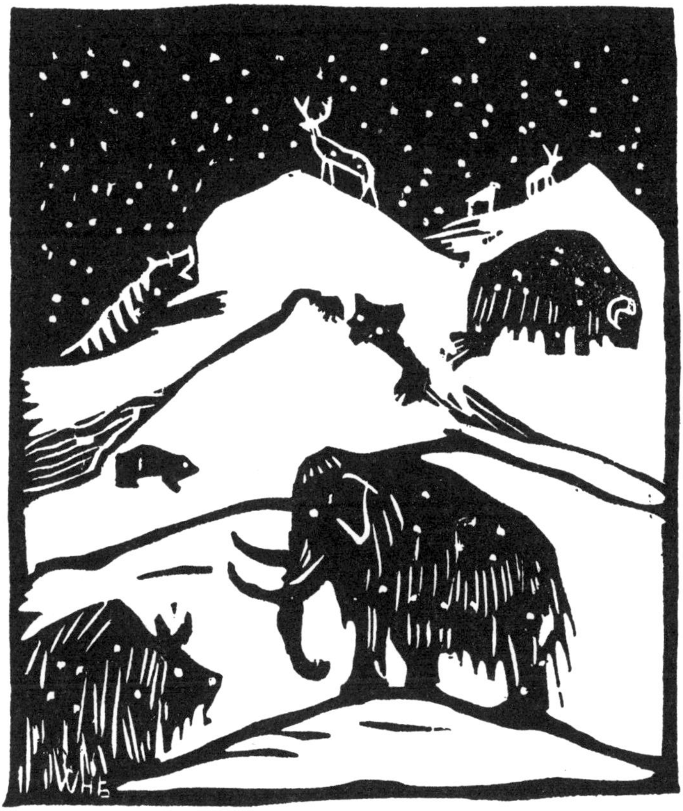

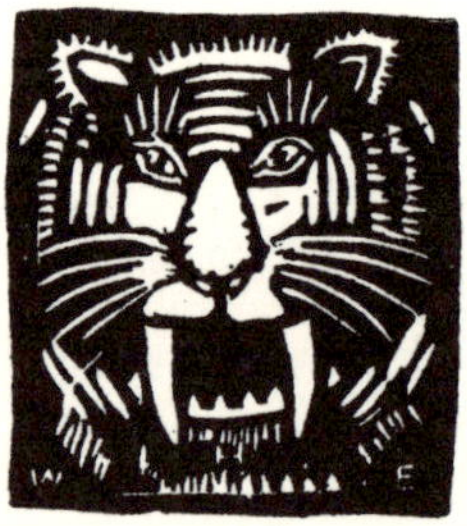

THE MAMMALS

(Eocene)

The reptiles laid eggs, and forgot all about them,
 And never took care of their young,
  Resembled the fishes,
  And kept all their wishes,
 For food and a place in the sun.

But the mammals appeared, and they set a new standard,
 They bore living babies, and so,
  They nursed them and fed them,
  They warmed them, and led them,
 And guarded, and helped them to grow.

The camels came on, and the wild e-o-hip-pus,
 The tapir, opossum, hedge-hog,
  In the old E-o-cene,
  Tigers, furry and lean,
 And wild packs of the primitive dog.

The monkeys appeared, and the grass-eating oxen,
 The branches of flesh-eating cat,
  The sheep, and the pig,
  (It was not very big)
 And I doubt if it often grew fat!

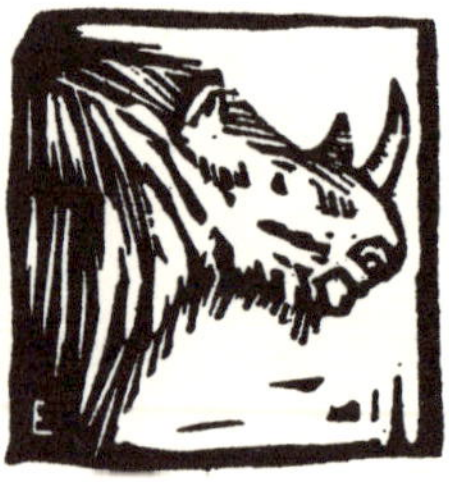

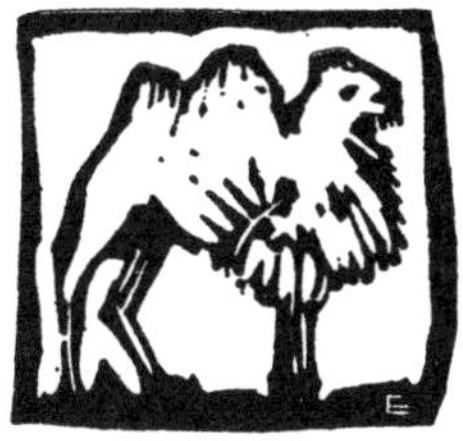

And soon there were birds with their feathered protection,
  Who watched over eggs in a nest,
    Till, birdies arriving,
    They fed them, contriving
  To teach them the ways that were best.

These warm-blooded creatures were very much wiser
  Than the former reptilian crew,
    With instinctive affection,
    Maternal protection,
  Instructed their little ones new.

And Oh! they were busy, for hunting and mating
  Meant ventures they never had known;
    And so through their fearings,
    Their bearing and rearings,
  Developed a brain of their own.

For brains are developed by seeing and doing,
  By living, and caring, and strife;
    They grow with our muscles,
    Through ventures and tussles,
  And all that we live in a life!

They do not fall down like the rains from the heavens,
  Which water the fields and the grains,
    'Tis just by diffusing,
    By living and using,
  That creatures grow wonderful brains!

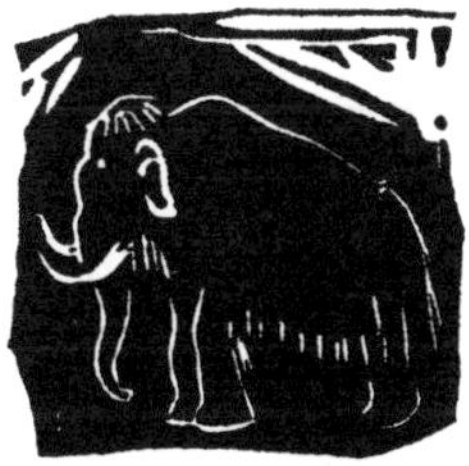

GEOGRAPHIC CHANGES

Put an orange on the shelf,
  And see the juices dry;
The skin grows loose, and puckers up,
  In wrinkles by and by.

Sometimes the mountains grow like this,
  And wrinkle up so far,
If folks had never climbed to see,
  We'd think they reached a star.

And in the ancient Me-o-cene,
  Came many mountain ranges,
Volcanoes; earthquakes cracked the land,
  Made geographic changes.

* * *

At last the mastadon appeared,
  His nose was three feet long;
He raised it upward like a horn,
  And trumpeted in song;

No bigger than a pony came
  Ancestors of the horse,
And flying deer, and every year,
  More monkey folks, of course.

Perhaps—some wild and hairy thing,
  That chattered with his clan,
And ambled queerly, used his hands,
  Well—something like a man!

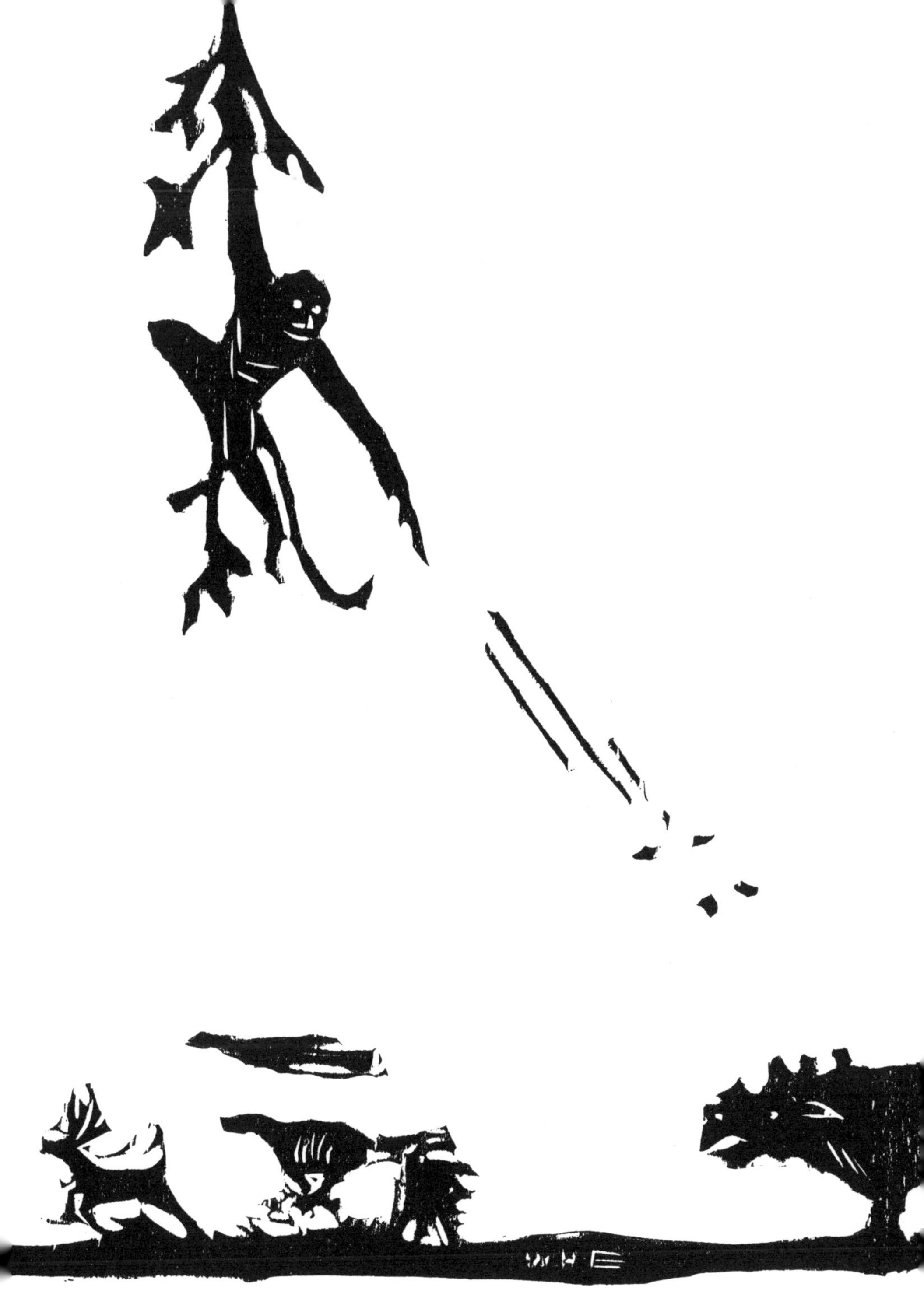

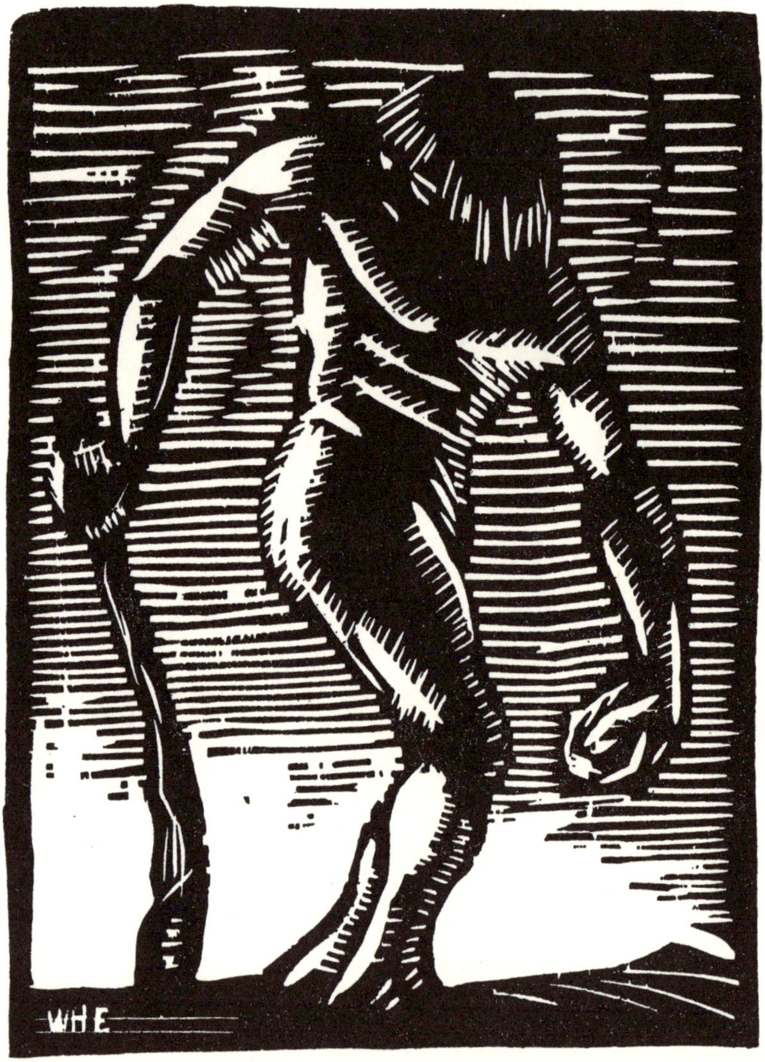

THE FIRST MAN

THE EARLY PITH-E-CAN-THRO-PUS

Before the time of cave men,
In the early Pli-o-cene,
There lived a pack of wild things,
All hairy, squat and lean;

They fought with tooth and sharp nails,
And wielded mighty stones;
That they walked as you and I do,
Is proven by their bones.

They had no tools or weapons;
They feared the fire too;
They hid, and skulked, and shivered,
As weaker creatures do.

They did not have a language;
Could scarcely speak at all,
But grunted sounds of portent,
Should good or ill befall.

They heard the tiger roar, when
He gorged upon his kill,
And when he had departed,
Crept out to eat their fill.

In wood, or swamp, or jungle,
Or out upon the plains,
They hurried forth in numbers,
And stole the grim remains.

And when they met a stranger,
They hit him on the head,
And ate, and ate, these cannibals,
Till all the pack was fed.

* * *

Perhaps a million years ago,
The human race began,
For the early pith-e-can-thro-pus
E-rect-us was a MAN!

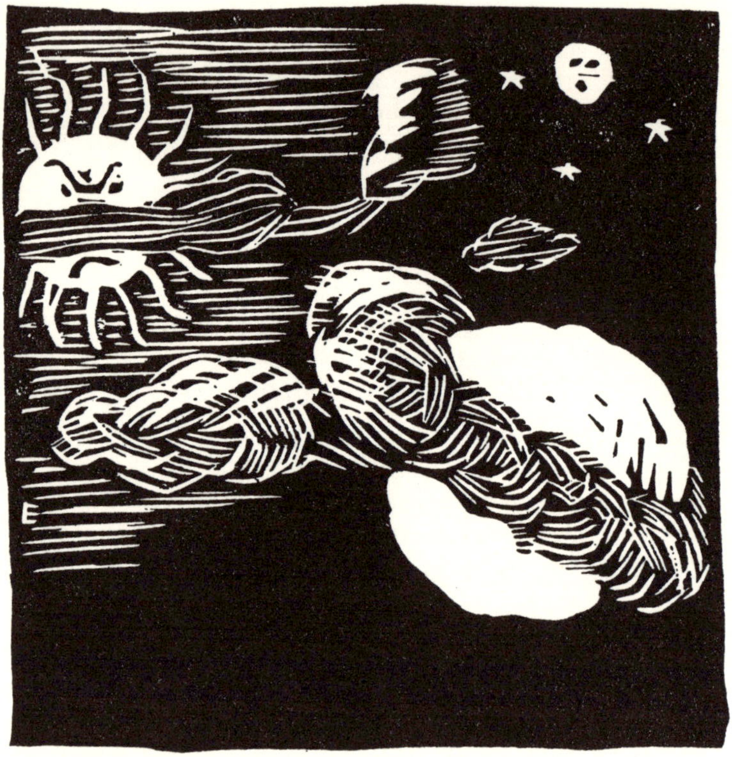

IN MIGHTY COSMIC RAGES

THE GLACIAL PERIOD

Portions of earth's surface cracked,
  And tumbled down inside;
The seas poured over in the holes,
  A swift and mighty tide.

Upon the furnace blazing there,
  Which spat in deadly fountains,
His streams of lava, ash and dust,
  Way up above the mountains.

With clouds of steam that filled the air,
  In mighty, cosmic rages,
That hid the sun and drove the rains,
  For weeks and months and ages.

And snows fell on the mountain tops,
  Gigantic glaciers forming,
Which slid and rumbled down the steeps,
  Demolishing and storming!

They covered all the land about,
  With sheets of ice and snow,
And made it very difficult
  For living things to grow!

(Note: Theory of glacial period advanced by Dr. M. Wilhelm Meyer, Prof. Hans Meyer of Leipsic, the brothers Sarasin of Basel and other eminent geologists.)

LIFE IN THE SNOWS

How did they live, the men,
  In those harsh days?
The beasts which throve
  In gentler ways?

In snowy huts,
  About the geyser's stream,
Which, boiling, spouted
  Plumes of steam?

Did thus men dwell?
  Or on the slopes
Of live volcanoes?
  Cherishing their hopes

Of lesser beasts
  Unfitted for the snows,
Which fell gaunt victims
  To old Hunger's throes?

Did thus men feed?
  And huddle through the years,
And wrap themselves in furs,
  And mock new fears?

Or were there lands
  Escaped the cold, where men
Survived and peopled
  Other lands again?

We know man lived,
  And fought, and won,
Till earth grew warm
  And he could greet the sun.

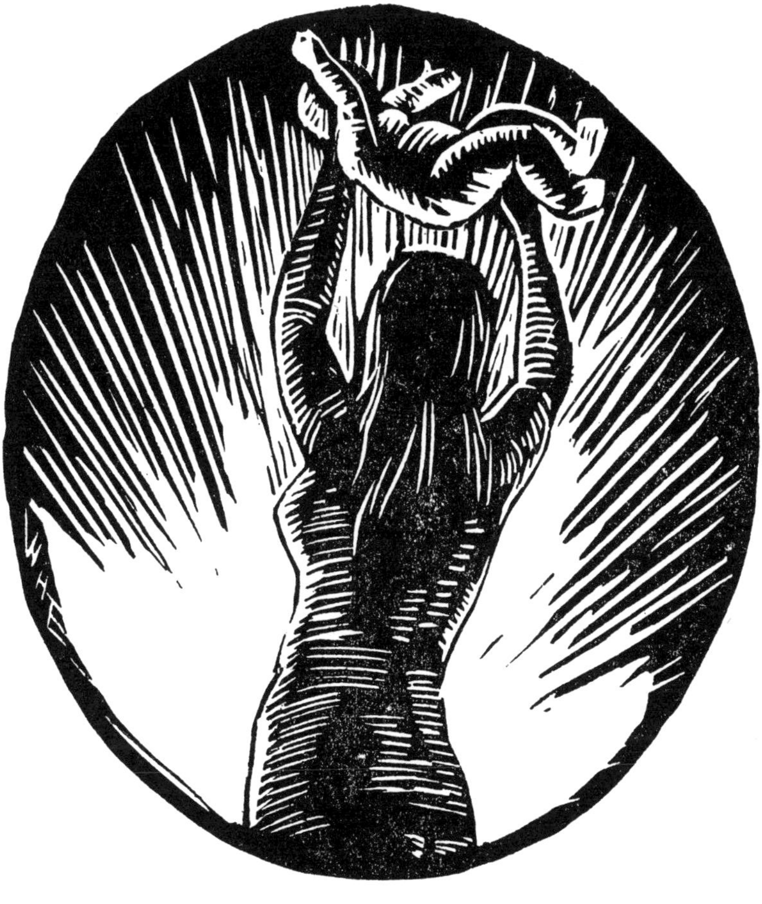

GREETING THE SUN

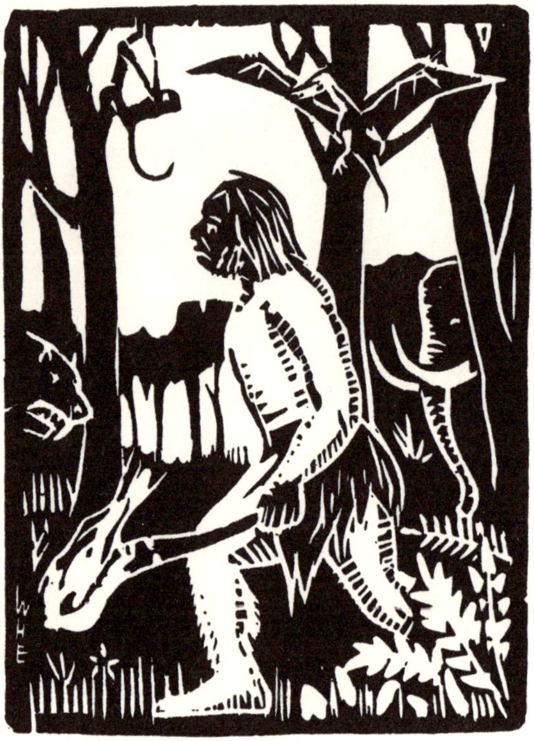

THE SAVAGE FOLK

Oh! Years and years and years ago,
  Before the day of books,
Before the age of towns and mills,
  Of grocery stores and cooks.

The world was filled with forests deep,
  And seas and rivers wide,
And here lived many savage tribes,
  And fearsome beasts beside.

The people slept in caves they found,
  Or brush huts daubed with clay,
Which were always rather leaky
  On a very rainy day.

And when the tiger, sabre-toothed,
  Came roaring through the wood,
The people trembled in their skins,
  And hid as best they could;

For if they tried to run away,
  This always meant disaster,
For tigers leap where men must run,
  And further far, and faster.

That strange and giant elephant,
  The mammoth thundered through
The woods, and trampled all he met,
  And ripped the trees in two.

The wild boar grunted in the swamp,
  And every gentle breeze
Carried the chatter from afar,
  Of monkeys in the trees.

And almost every savage beast
  Had longer fangs to tear,
And swifter feet than puny man,
  And menaced everywhere.

And so men learned to wait and watch,
  When beasts would eat and drink;
Learned to outwit the stronger foe,
  To see, and plan, and THINK.

And here are rhymes of how they lived,
  When man was just begun,
Of how the weak became the strong,
  And fought, and learned, and WON!

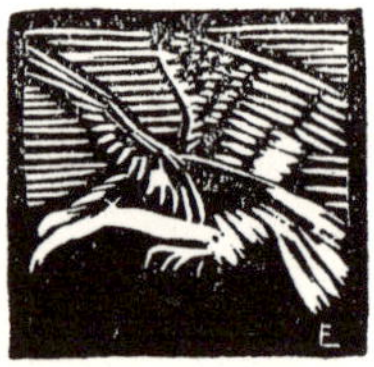

THE FOREST FIRE

The cave folks feared
When the wild winds blew,
In their primitive ways,
In the old, old days;
They shivered and hid
When the black clouds grew,
And the thunder roared,
And the brown leaves flew,
When the lightning crashed,
And the tall woods blazed,
And the red fire ran
Till the trees were razed.

Then all the beasts
Ran away in fright,
Helter and skelter
With all their might;
The gold bees bumbled,
The elephants stumbled,
All brutes were jumbled
In one mad flight.

The cave folks scattered,
And ran and hid,
And chattered much
As the monkeys did;
Till the rains came down,
And the fire fell,
They watched from afar
And saw all was well.

But the wild beasts stopped
In their race with Fear,
And their Stomachs said:
"There is fresh meat here";
While their tearing claws,
And their slashing jaws,
Startled the people
Afar and near.

But the cave folks held
All their foes at bay,
With the flaming branches
They seized one day.
They learned the blaze
Was a faithful friend,
That he held them safe
When the brutes would rend.

They learned to feed him;
Through night and day,
He was watched and coaxed
To keep foes away;
For matches and flint
Were not thereabout,
And the grey wolves came
When the flames died out.
When the flames died out,
For they knew no way
To kindle a blaze
In that far off day.

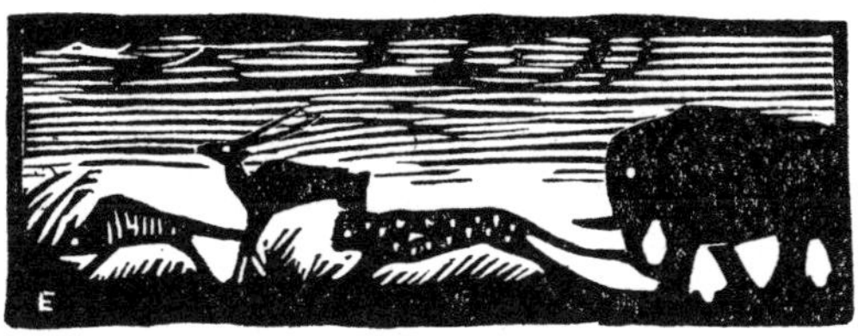

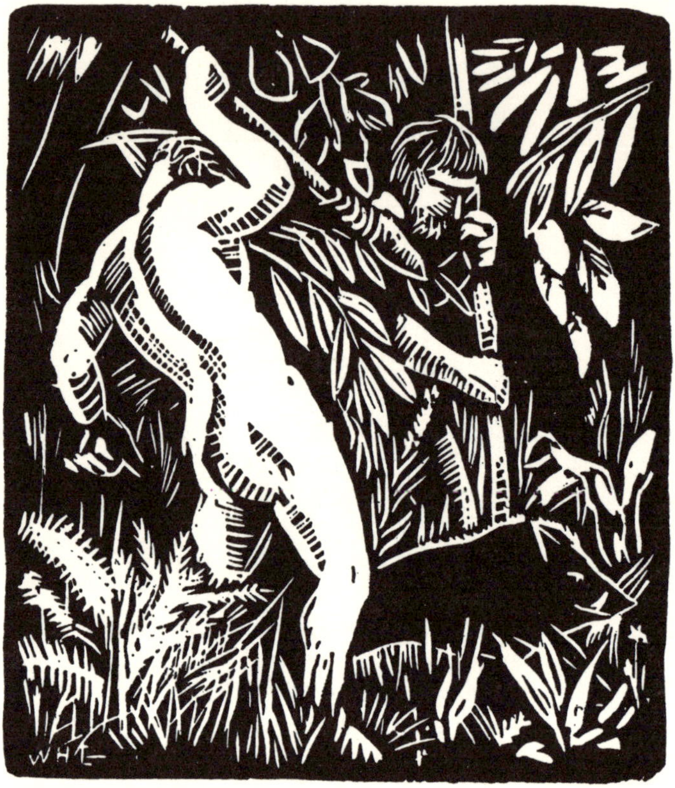

KILLED A WILD BOAR

EMPTY AS A BUBBLE

Little Fish, the cave boy,
  Was empty as a bubble;
He sucked the bones of bear toes,
  And made his elders trouble.

The men were gone a-hunting,
  With sharpened spears of bone;
They found and killed a wild boar,
  A-rooting all alone.

They bore him back in triumph,
  Hacked up the dripping beast,
And round the blazing fires,
  They held a noble feast.

They never thought to cook him,
  But ate him raw and red,
And laughed and chewed in comfort,
  Till all the tribe was fed.

They heard the wild beasts prowling;
  They heard the tiger creep,
And crawled into their cave homes,
  And soon were fast asleep,

Save one who fed the fire,
  Who watched till break of day,
To hold the tribe in safety,
  And keep the wolves away.

THE ELEPHANT'S TRUNK

The animal's neck was so thick and short,
  He could not reach down to eat
The succulent grass of the rolling plains,
  Nor the bamboo young and sweet.

The animal's tusks were so long and sharp,
  They curved like an ancient sword;
And many the lions he ripped and rent,
  When he slashed and tore and gored.

This primitive beast had a long soft nose
  And he thrust it all about;
He wiggled it and woggled it; he jiggled it and joggled it,
  And picked food with his snout.

He stretched his snout when he wanted a peach,
  And he frequently filled his nose,
With water and emptied it into his mouth,
  Like a fat, round, rubber hose.

He reached and he stretched for the ripe brown nuts,
  Till his snout grew thick and strong,
And he stretched, and he reached for the fresh young
      blooms,
  Till—his nose was ten feet long!

* * *

And that's how the animal changed his face,
  And the elephant came to grow,
With a trunk that could pick and tear for him,
  In the long, long, long ago!

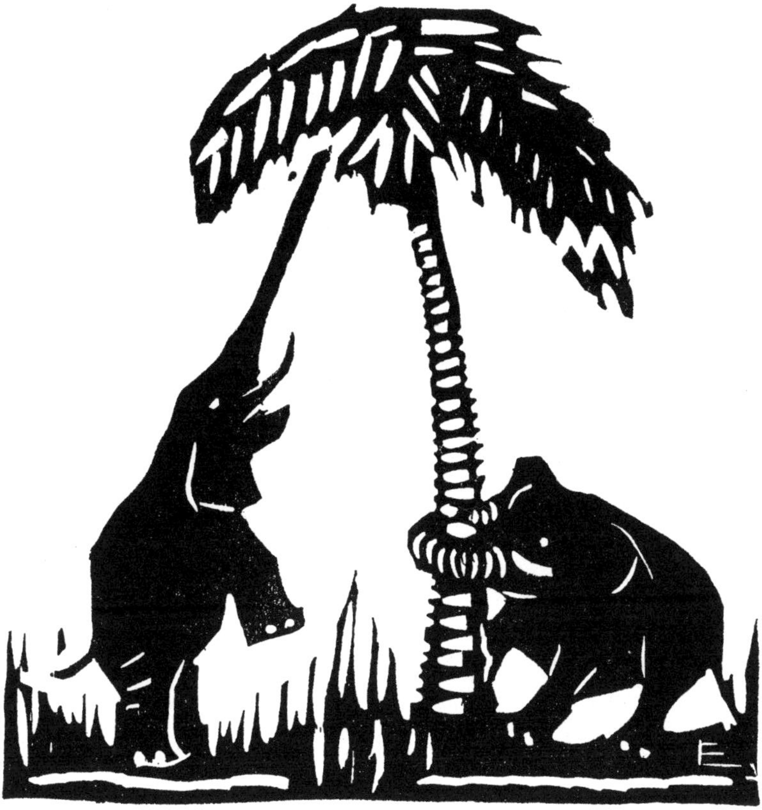

HE STRETCHED FOR THE RIPE BROWN NUTS

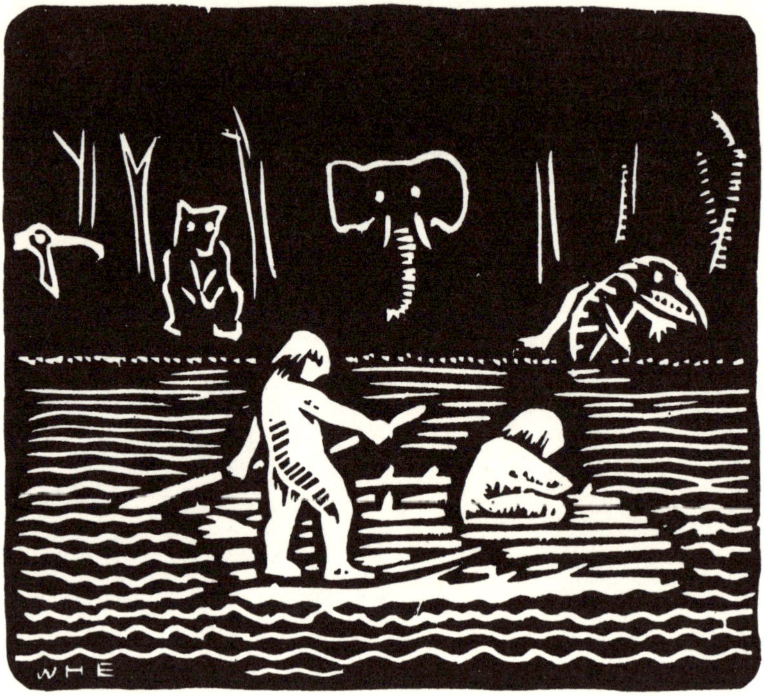

MADE A RAFT AS CHILDREN DO

THE RAFT

(On a river emptying into the sea)

The fibrous plants, and bark and things
The cave folks stripped and used as strings;

By braiding fibres in and out,
They wove a rope surprising stout;

With ax of stone they chopped bamboo,
And made a raft, as children do,

Of many poles, securely tied;
And launched their raft to take a ride.

The river current bore them past
Familiar places far and fast.

No sail to catch the winds that blow,
They had no oars with which to row,

And so they slowly swam to shore,
And towed the raft a mile, or more;

Then chopped a pole to push and guide,
As they rode homeward on the tide.

CUT-CUT-CUT-CA-DAWK-IT!

(Note: Biologists tell us that years and years ago chickens were wild birds, the hens laying their eggs but once a year—in the spring. Since their domestication, man has, by preserving the best layers, and by experiments in foods, etc., etc., produced a hen which will lay all the year. Biologists also inform us that hens fly from their nests cackling wildly when beasts appear, in order to draw the enemy away from their eggs.)

Children playing in the trees,
  Branches swaying, bending;
Leaping, climbing in the breeze,
  Laughter never-ending,

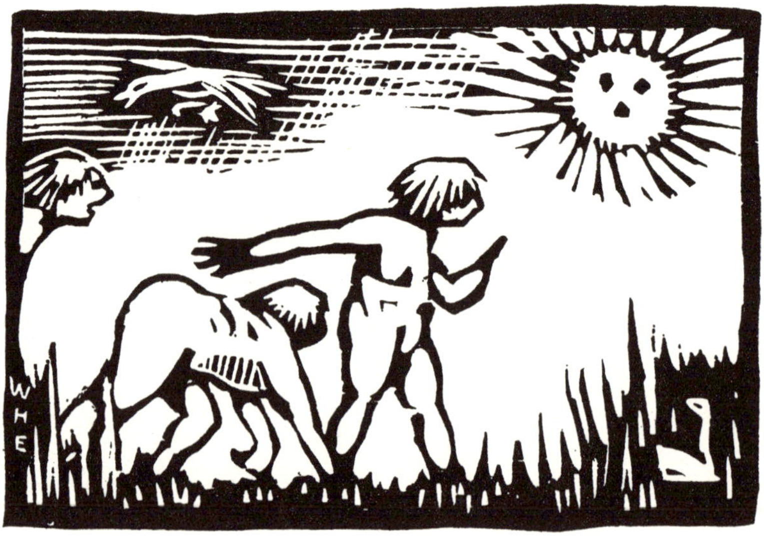

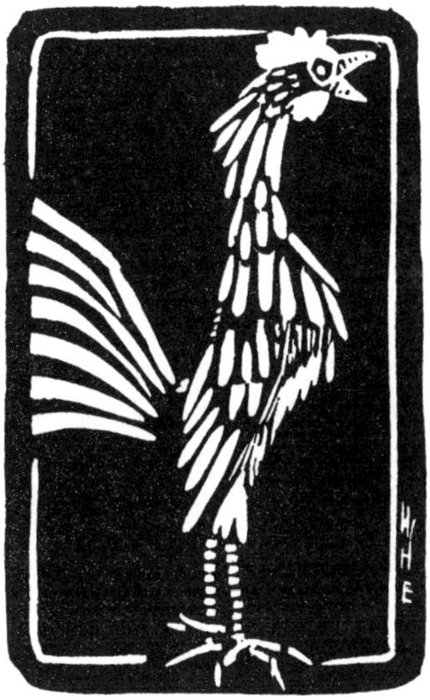

Hushed their songs to hunt for eggs,
  Softly all together,
Hands and arms and feet and legs,
  Silent as a feather!

Gave the mother bird a fright,
  When a dead leaf crackled,
Mother chicken in a plight,
  Flew above and cackled;

Drew the children far away,
  "Tawk-it! Tawk-it! Tawk-it!"
From her nest of twigs and clay,
  "Cut-cut-cut-ca-dawk-it!"

Knew they hunted for her nest;
  (Where a boy who does not?)
Did her prehistoric best,
  To lead them where it was not.

Brown eggs hidden in the grass,
  Safe as any flower,
Racing, climbing children pass,
  Like a summer shower.

Far above the mothers fly,
  With a ceaseless squawking,
Saving future chickens by
  "Cut-cut-cut-ca-dawk-ing."

THE LITTLE EOHIPPUS

The little eohippus
Was a prehistoric horse;
He roamed the plains
A million years ago!
    Go! Go!
He loved to eat the grasses
Growing sweet and tall and coarse,
And he ran as fast
As any startled doe!
    Doe! Doe!
        He galloped on the hilltops,
        And he pranced upon the plains;
        He strutted
        Though he wasn't very tall,
            Tall, Tall;
        He loved the summer sunshine,
        And he liked the driving rains;
        In a race
        He often beat his fellows all,
            All, all!
                The little eohippus grew
                From one foot high to four,
                In a hundred thousand years
                Or more, they say,
                    Say, Say;
                He ran a hundred miles a day,
                Sometimes he galloped more,
                And he frolicked like the colts,
                That learn to play,
                    Play, play.
                        Four toes he had on his fore feet,
                        And three on those behind;
                        He watched the monkeys
                        Swinging in the trees,
                            Trees, trees;
                        He never killed the smaller beasts,
                        His appetites were kind,
                        And—he sniffed a thousand odors
                        On the breeze,
                            Breeze, breeze.

One day while swinging earthward,
On a very shaky limb,
A cave boy fell,
And landed all astride,
    Stride, stride
A little eohippus
And the tumble jolted him,
But he had a most surprising
Pony ride,
    Ride, ride.

The little eohippus
Was as frightened as the boy,
And Oh! the boy was feeling
Very pale,
    Pale, pale!
The pony tried to throw him,
With a sudden savage joy,
But the boy clung on,
And clutched his mane and tail,
    Tail, tail!

The little eohippus ran
Until his legs grew weak;
He stumbled
And his gait began to slack,
    Slack, slack;
And Oh! but he was thirsty
And astonishingly meek,
For he thought he had a monkey
On his back,
    Back, back!

And when he found the tribe folks,
The cave boy told with pride,
How swinging on a limb
He had a fall,
    Fall, fall,
How he landed on the pony,
Had an eohippus ride,
And declared
That he was never scared at all,
    All, all.

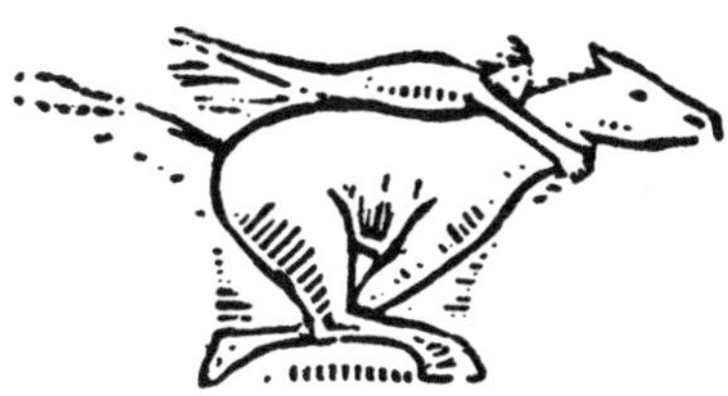

LOST

The Stomach of O Wah Lee plead:
  "I want to eat! To eat!"
The Nostrils of O Wah Lee said:
  "The air is sweet! Is sweet!
"There isn't any foe about;
"There lurks no beast for folks to rout;
"I think we'd better venture out,
  "To eat! To eat! To eat!"

She wriggled through the waving grass,
  That none might bid her stay;
And ran behind a tangled mass,
  Till she was far away.
She thought: I'm sure if I insist,
I'll find a nest if I persist,
And kill a hen if she resist,
  And eat my fill to-day.

She heard a whining panther cub,
  And saw a tiny pair
Of brownie bunnies in the wood,
  And here and yon and there,
She found fresh eggs discreetly hid
Where grasses grow the oaks amid,
And sucked them as her elders did,
  Which made the monkeys stare.

She picked the berries fat and red,
  And ate them as she would;

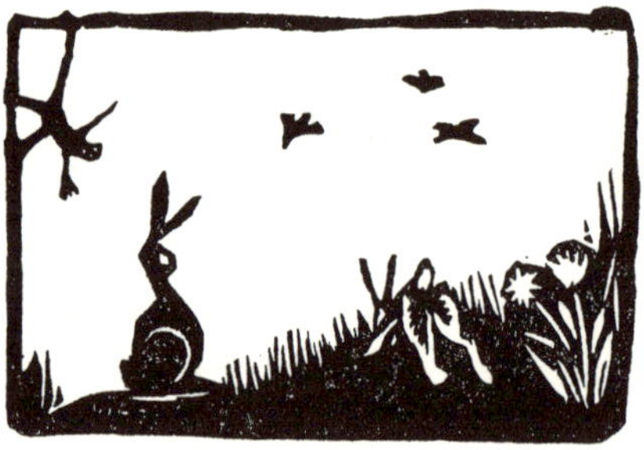

And tubers in their earthy bed,
She dug as best she could;
She chased a flying porcupine,
Who flipped his quills with cool design,
To say: "Begone! The woods are mine."
O Wah Lee understood.

But when she saw approaching dark,
Her heart began to yearn,
For any kind, familiar mark
To show her where to turn;
Remembered things the Cave Folks taught
Too late, so they availed her not;
She had indeed the way forgot,
And wanted to return.

She heard a hissing snake, but when
She swung herself on high,
The branches of an oak tree, then
A panther flitted by;
But she was huddled out of sight,
Her scent was borne exactly right;
She silent clung; her breath was light
As summer winds that sigh.

At last she heard a welcome sound,
The tribe was searching near;
And she was happy when it found
A youngster stark with fear;
But flaring torches in the dark,
And blessed fire's magic spark,
Adventure made a joyous lark,
And hungry jackals peer.

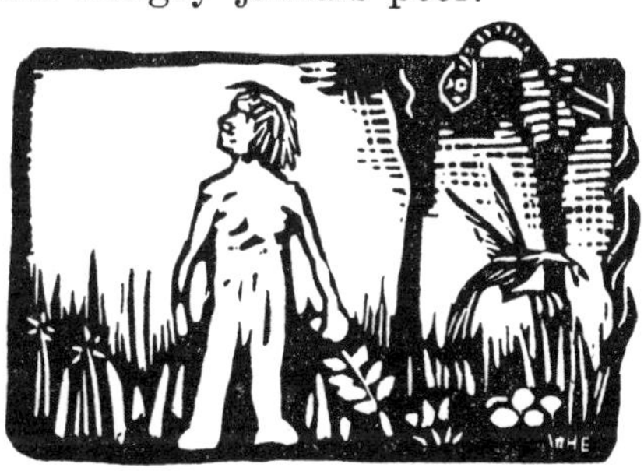

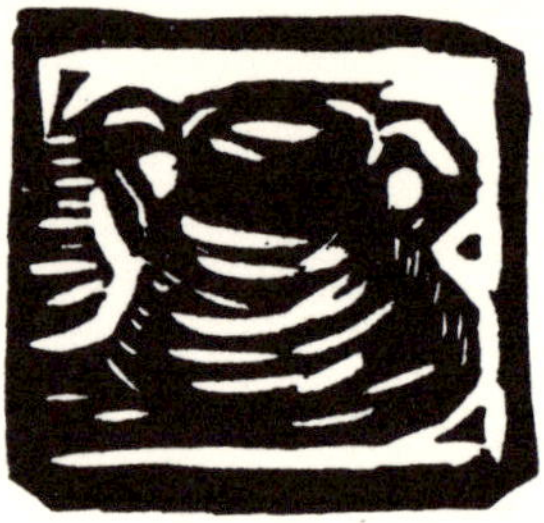

WAH TEE MADE A BOWL

Wah Tee wove a basket,
  With many twists and passes,
(To carry eggs and berries in)
  Of brown and yellow grasses.

The basket carried nuts and shells,
  And fruit and snails and fishes,
For in that far off long ago,
  There weren't any dishes.

And when the rainy season passed,
  And days grew long and hotter,
Wah Tee regretted that his basket
  Would not carry water.

He lined and covered it with clay,
  And in a corner sunny,
He hung his basket up to dry,
  And ran to gather honey.

And all day long the sun shone down,
  And warmed and cooked, and caked it,
And made the basket tight and strong,
  And hardened it and baked it.

So now the basket was a bowl,
  And carried cooling water,
And all the people looked and learned
  Of Wah Tee Wee, the potter.

So all the cave folks gathered clay,
  And hands obeyed the wishes
Of squatting people learning to
  Make pots, and bowls and dishes!

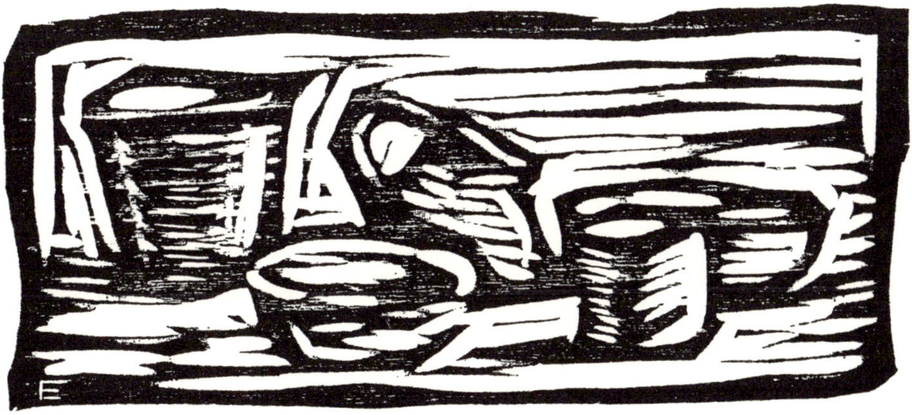

THE NOSE OF A BEAR.

A wonderful guide is the Nose of a bear,
It reads him the news that is borne on the air;

It tells him the tigress is hunting to-day
For her fluffy young cubs hidden safely away;

It says: "Better feed in the valley below,
"Or the witchity swamp where the blue-berries grow;

"Descend the ravine where the brambles are thick;
"The brute's coming closer; you'd better move quick!"

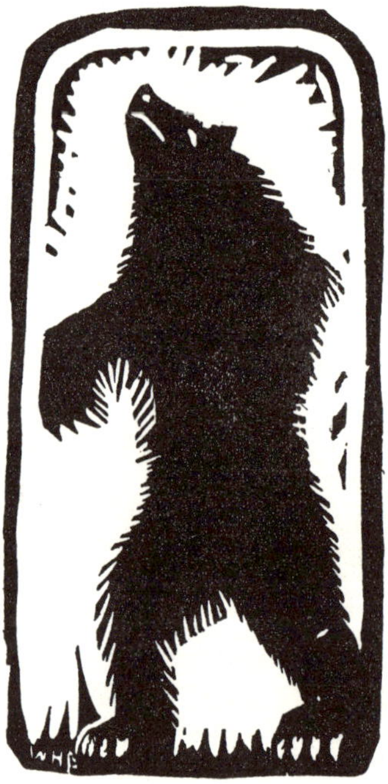

And bruin obeys with his Nose for a guide,
And hurries along in his lumbering stride,

Till his Nostrils declare: "I've the scent of a deer,
"If the tigress attacks him, you've nothing to fear.

"There are succulent plums hanging thick from the bough,
"But I warn, do not stop to examine them now.

"When the tigress goes home with her kill, maybe then,
"I will show you the way to return here again.

"The moss by the river is tender and clean,
"The plants in the hollow are juicy and green."

And bruin ran on in his lumbering stride,
Though he wanted to pause for the sweets at his side.

"But wait!" said his Nose, "where the breezes are free,
"And I'll tell you the news if you listen to me.

"There is blood in the wind, for the tigress has slain,
"You have need to be cautious returning again!

"The odor of plums is enticingly sweet;
"Go back to the trees and have something to eat;

"And I will keep watch till I read in the air,
"That the tigress has fed and returned to her lair."

* * * * * * * *

Oh! The Nose of a bear is a wonderful friend,
For it leads him, and feeds him sweet grubs without end!

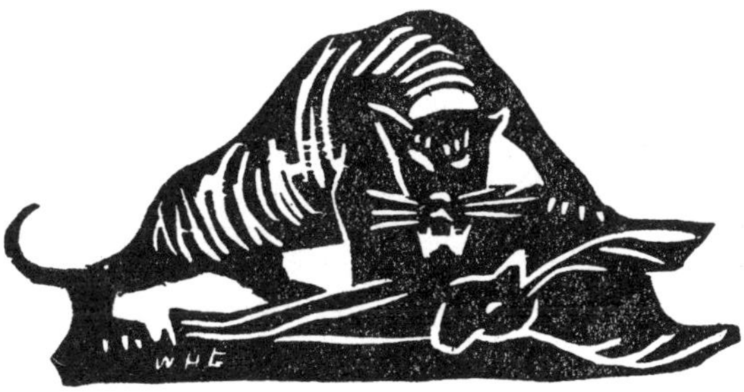

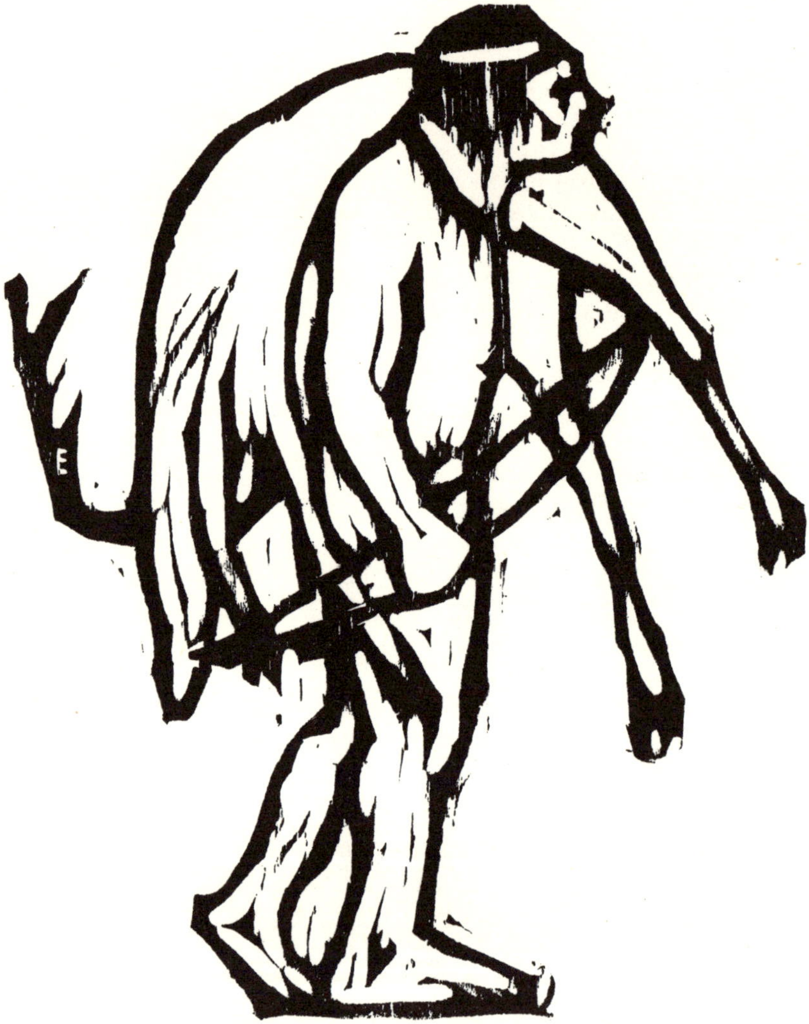

ORNAMENTS

OO-Tah-Ta killed a cobra,
  And wore her skin to tell
The tribe that he had served it
  Most astonishingly well.

Wow-wow-wow—had two wolf tails
  Enbraided in his hair,
As tokens of his prowess,
  And he wore them everywhere.

Me-fah-la made a necklace
  Of teeth and ears and bone,
Reminders of his skill
  With bow and arrows tipped with stone.

The breast of Running Water
  Bore his self-inflicted slashes,
That all might know a cave man
  Who laughed at pain and gashes.

Ne-o-nee wore a deer skin,
  The squatting folks to charm,
And when the days were rainy,
  He found it kept him warm.

The Warbler stole the deer skin,
  When none was by to note,
And cut it with a flint knife,
  To make her son a coat.

She punched it full of eyelets,
  Made with a bony prong,
And fitted it securely,
  And laced it with a thong.

The Swift One wore the new coat,
  And never felt the rain,
And often wished the Warbler
  Would go hunting deer again.

THE KANGAROO

This is a song
Of the kangaroo,
Who carried her young
In a manner new;
In a pocket of skin,
They were all tucked in,
In a wee, warm apron
Down under her chin.

But this gentle beast
Was unfit to claw,
Or fight for her cubs
With a sabre jaw;
But her eyes were keen
For the welcome sheen
On the toothsome shoots,
Growing young and green.

She was soft and weak,
And her teeth were small;
She could never be queen
Of the forest at all;
While her ears took care,
With her nose aware,
She feasted and filled
Where the bulbs were rare.

She feasted and filled,
But when danger came,
She bounded away
Like a dancing flame;
Leaped over a spring
With a mighty swing,
And vanished as swift
As the wild birds wing.

And none could o'ertake her,
The kangaroo,
Who carried her young
In a manner new;
In a pocket of skin
They were all tucked in,
In a wee, warm apron.
Down under her chin.

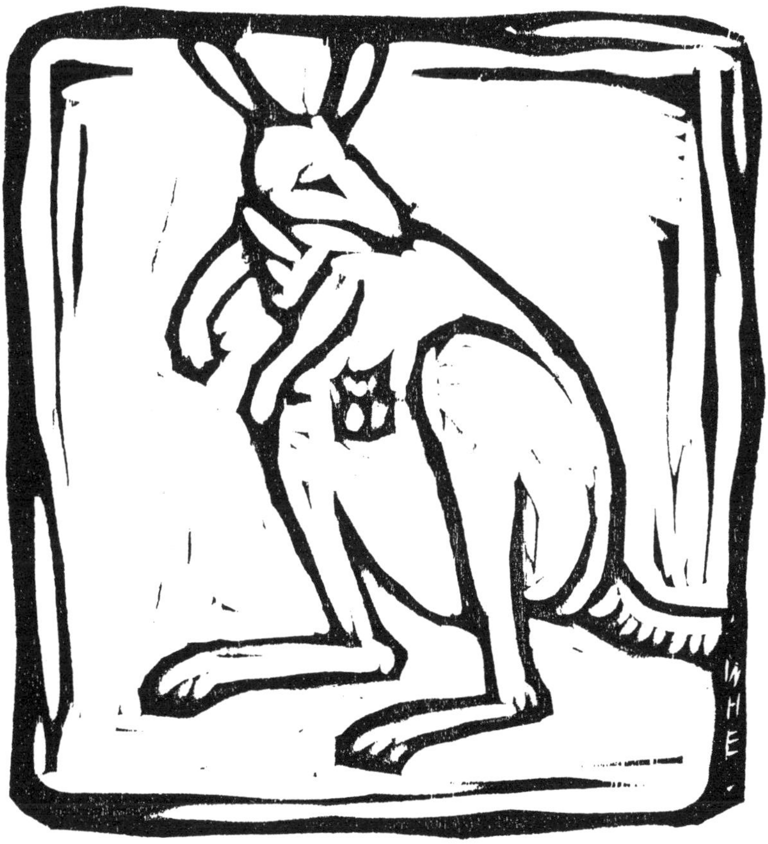

KNIVES AND CUPS

To-to found a flint pit,
  The pit was full of treasure,
Of long flakes and strong flakes,
  A very goodly measure.

To-to chipped the flint flakes,
  Till they grew sharp and thinner,
And made a half a dozen knives,
  For folks to cut their dinner.

Stone knives and flint knives,
  For carving meat and fishes;
Red bowls of clay rolls,
  And clumsy earthen dishes.

Short horns and sea shells,
  The cave folks boasted, thinking,
That never had the world before,
  Such fancy cups for drinking!

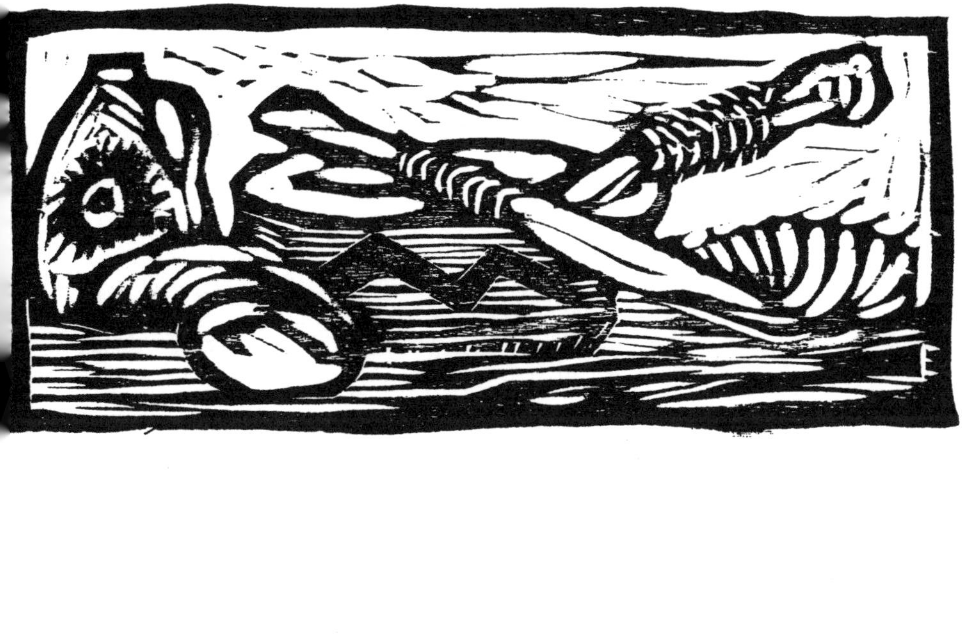

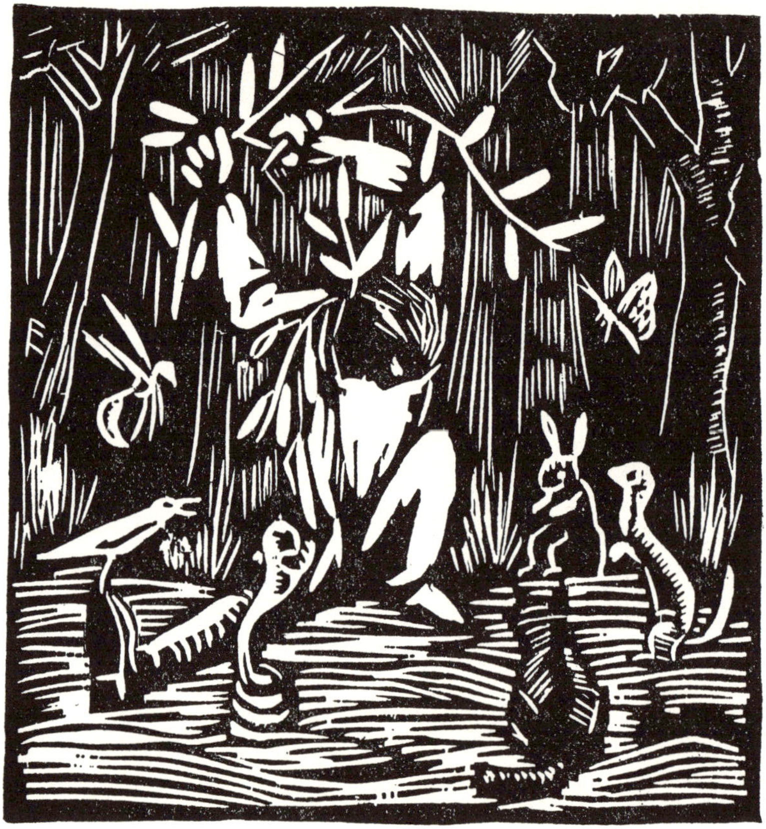

IMITATE A STUMP

RABBITS WHITE AND BROWN

(Note: If elders will look up Darwin or any other biologist on "Protective Coloration" they will find ample material for enlarging on this theme to the enjoyment of themselves as well as the youngsters.)

White rabbits in the wood,
  Are like soft balls of snow,
But foxes hunting dinner
  See them everywhere they go.

Brown bunnies in the woods,
  As saucy as you please,
Are safer far from foxes,
  They look so like the trees.

This is why in wild spots,
  The white hares disappear,
And brown hares hide in safety
  When hunting folks appear.

And this is why in snow-lands,
  The bunnies all are white;
For hunters see the brown ones,
  And take them home at night.

So if you're in a wild land,
  Don't run, or sing, or jump,
But wear a coat of brown stuff,
  And imitate a stump;

So creatures cannot see you.
  They'll think you are a tree;
So silent as a moon beam,
  Be safe as safe may be!

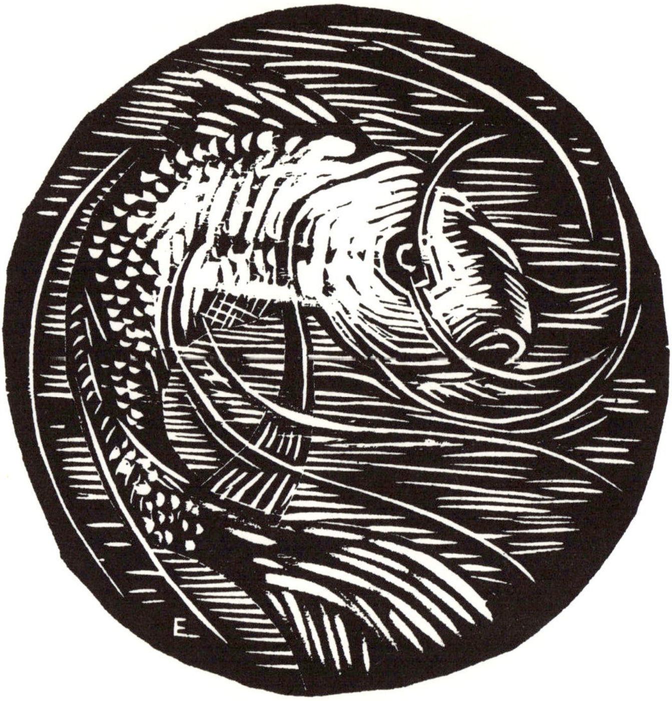

FISHING

Spearing fish is lots of fun,
  Gigging fish for dinner,
While the flying dragons hum,
  Stomachs growing thinner.

Softly searching near the shore,
  Where the willow brushes,
For the shy and speckled prize,
  Hidden in the rushes.

What a lot of water things!
  Scaly folks, and finny,
Darting with their water wings,
  Like a giant minnie.

Oh! The gold and silver scale,—
  Hold your weapon ready,
While he flirts his slender tail—
  Steady! Steady! Steady!

See the muddied waters churn,
  O but he's a flopper!
Drag him out and you shall learn
  You have caught a whopper!

Water snake and jumping frog,
  Here's an alligator,
Floating toward you like a log,
  Vicious imitator!

String them on a willow pole—
  Stomachs growing thinner—
Red and gold and speckled fish,
  What a dainty dinner!

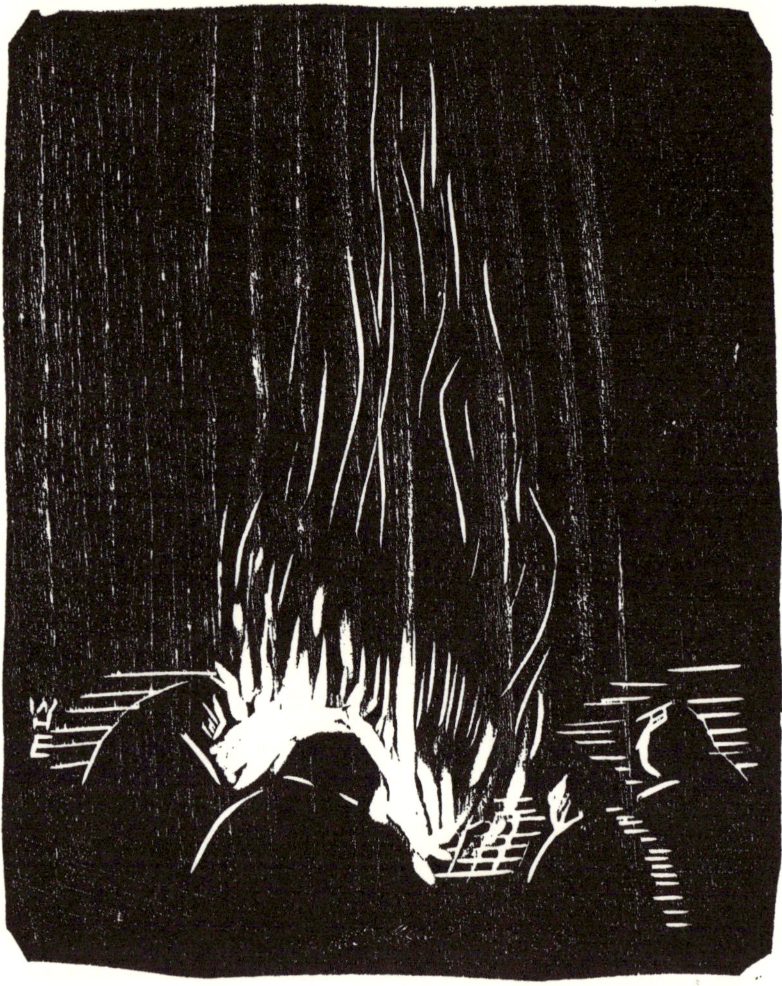

THERE WAS A FIRE

LITTLE TOE STUMBLED

Back to the caves again,
  Jiggity jog,
Little Toe slipped
  And fell over a log!

There was a fire,
  The fishes fell in it,
And nobody saved them
  For over a minute!

The cave people grumbled;
  They thought they were spoiled;
They never had eaten fish,
  Roasted or broiled.

But all were so hungry
  They squatted to sup,
And tasted, and liked them,
  And gobbled them up!

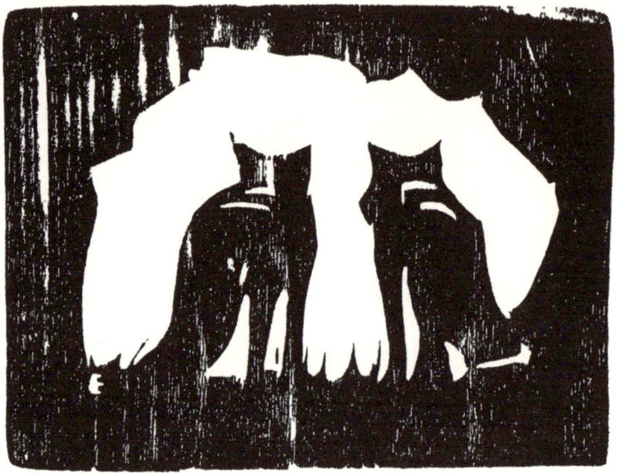

THE DINGO

Two little wolf cubs,
  Snarling, romping, shunting,
Nipping brother on the ear;
  Mother's gone a-hunting.

Three hungry wolf whelps,
  Peevish, snarling, whining,
Watch for mother in the cave,
  Yellow eyes and shining.

Three little cross cubs,
  Stomachs growing flatter,
Scratch and quarrel and grumble—
  Wonder what's the matter.

Three little lone whelps,
  Darker shadows creeping,—
Crinkled nose, and snuggled toes,—
  Whimper in their sleeping.

One little brown cub,
  Fear and danger scorning,
Wants her mother; wanders out
  To find her in the morning.

One falling cocoanut,
  Makes her start and cower,
While a frightened mother bird
  Causes her to glower.

Timidly she creeps on,
  Night-jars chatter pertly,
When they flap away in flight,
  Hides herself alertly.

Stumbles over big feet,
  Poking, sniffing, smelling,
What a lot of wonder things
  Busy Nose is telling!

Little Toe with basket,
  Heard her frightened yelping,
Found a thorn in small paw,
  Gave a kindly helping.

Put her in the basket,
  Baby teeth were biting,
But she hadn't learned of
  Savage, wolfish fighting.

Little Toe ran caveward,
  Fearful of her mother,
When she fought and howled,
  Sought her cries to smother.

One little brown wolf,
  Lost her temper snappy;
Folks fed her lumps of meat;
  Tame she grew, and happy.

One friendly brown wolf,
  People called her "Dingo",
Learned to guard the folks at night,
  Like the farmer's "Bingo".

This restless wolf-dog,
  Ran away one season;
Hid herself within a cave;
  Can you guess the reason?

Four little cave folks,
  Yielded supper sadly,
When Dingo wandered back to beg,
  And ate their portions gladly.

Four happy cave boys!
  People couldn't find her—
But Dingo wandered home again—
  With little pups behind her!

* * *

You have a watch dog, and
  This little rhyme is dinning
The fact that dingo guarded
  When the tribes were just beginning.

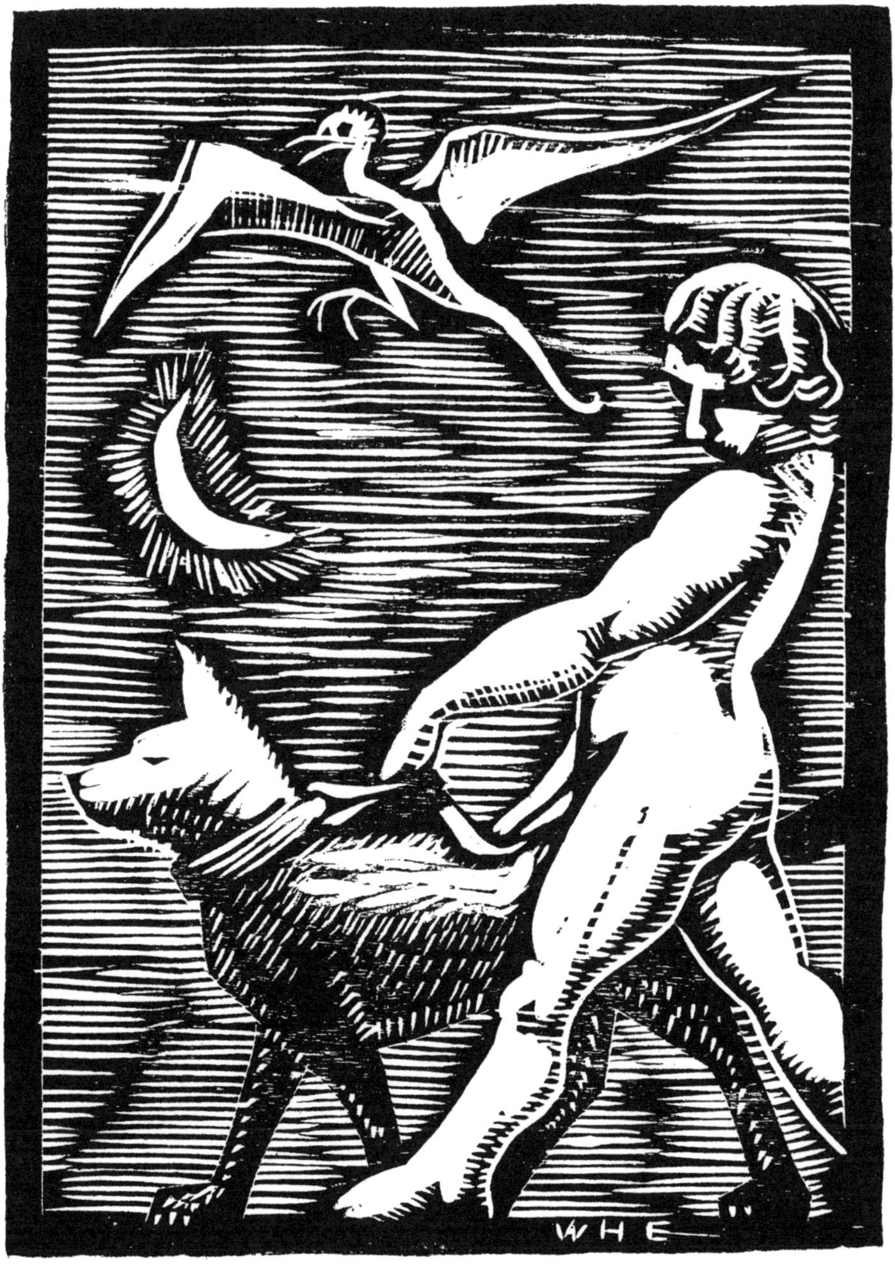
WHE

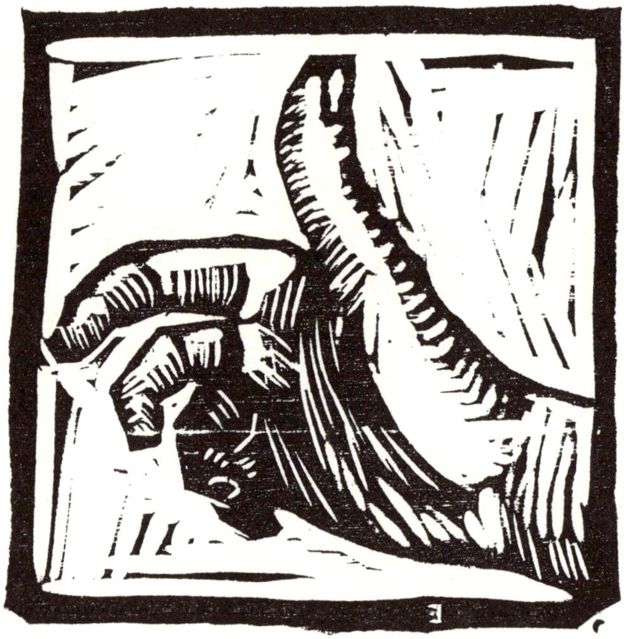

O WHAT WOULD WE DO WITHOUT THUMBS?

Thumbs! Thumbs!
O what could we do without thumbs?
  We couldn't do baking,
  Nor building, nor raking,
We couldn't play fiddles or drums!

Dear! Dear!
We would be very awkward, I fear!
  We couldn't do sowing,
  Nor digging, nor rowing;
O wouldn't the people seem queer!

My! My!
And how could we eat apple pie?
  Or wipe off our noses,
  Or button our clotheses?
We would be like the dogs—you and I!

For—For—
We could not even open a door,
  Nor play ball for pleasure,
  Nor weigh things, nor measure—
Why—we wouldn't be FOLKS any more!

Drums! Drums!
The key to a mystery comes!
  The Cave Folks could beat them,
  The foes that would eat them—
Because they had fingers and thumbs!

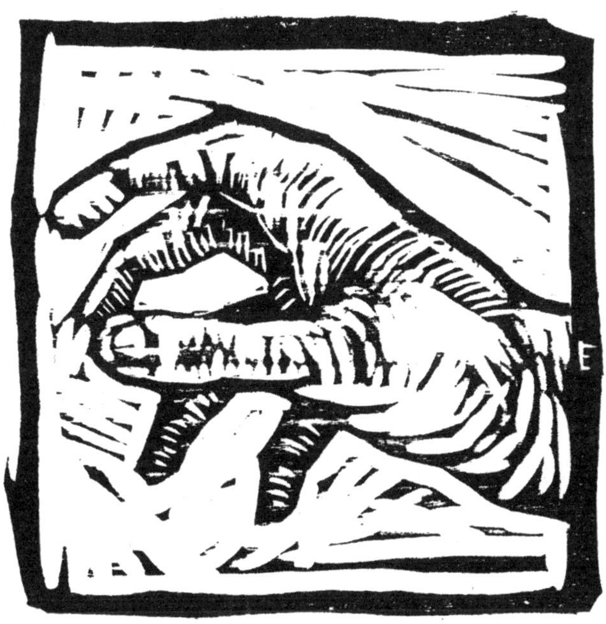

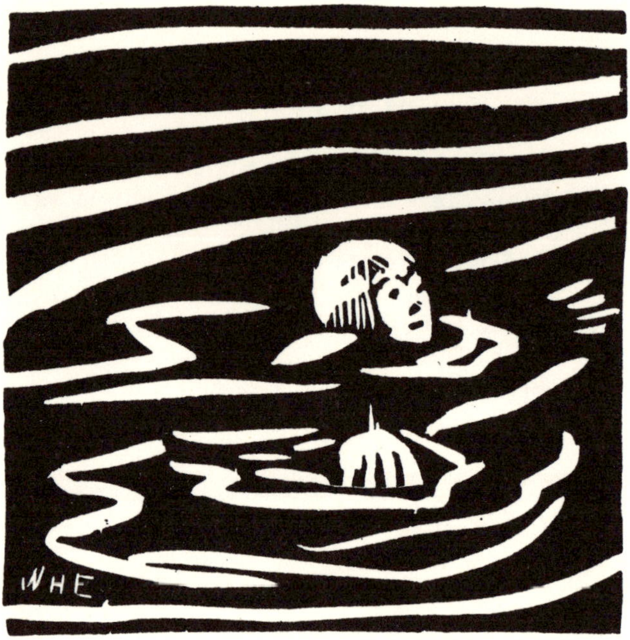

SWIMMING

The boys and girls straddled
A log, and they paddled,
With all of their hands
And their feet;
They balanced and held him;
They pulled and propelled him;
And Oh! But the splashing
Was sweet!

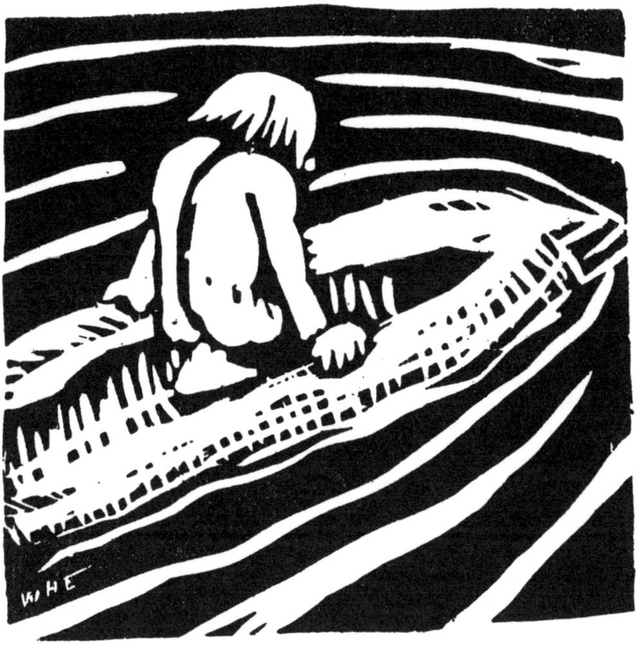

But it isn't much wonder,
The children went under,
  Without any warning
    At all,
When, the log rolling over,
A bobbing sea-rover,
  Upset them and gave them
    A fall!

They dived and they stuttered,
They swam and they sputtered,
  And laughed at the slap
    Of a wave;
But Oh! How he pleased them!
And ducked them and teased them!
  He could never be taught
    To behave!

Then, swimming, they followed
A log that was hollowed
  By fires that burn
    In the trees;
They did not bestride it;
But tumbled inside it;
  'Twas almost a boat,
    If you please.

Of course it was tippy,
And clumsy and dippy;
  It was half under water
    As well,
But they filled up the places
Where the water ran races,
  And made it as tight
    As a bell!

And so while deriving,
When swimming and diving,
  The manners of waters,
    And floats,
They later, by burnings,
And choppings, and turnings,
  Learned how to make logs
    Into boats!

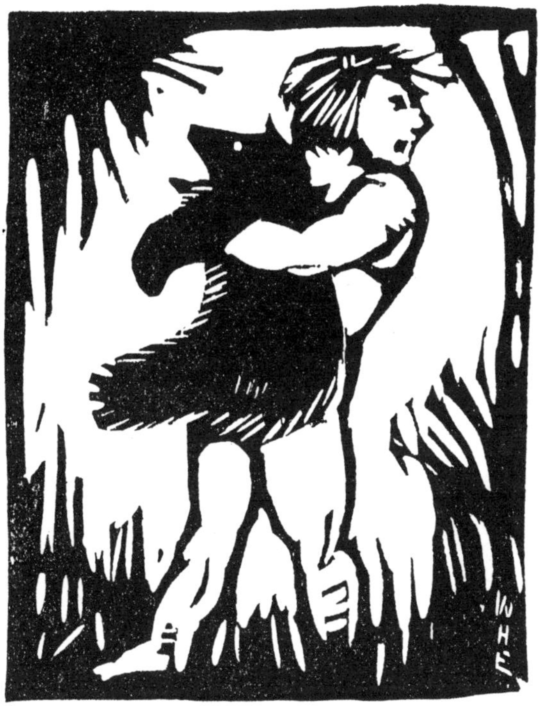

THE BEAR CUB

The pea-fowl and sea-fowl
  Were lazy and frowzy,
The plumes of the bamboo
  Were nodding and drowsy;
The river was purple,
  And golden and silk,
And Hoto was thirsty
  For cocoa-nut milk.

A thousand sweet odors
  Were borne on the breeze,
But all seemed to whisper—
  Of cocoa-nut trees;

So Hoto sped on
  Till he came to a tangle,
Where ferns nestle deep,
  And the moss streamers dangle;

He heard a low squeal,
  And his footsteps arrested,
Before him a bear cub
  The pathway contested;
A little black cub,
  Which was frightened and chunky,
And scampered as droll
  As a capering monkey.

She felt herself lifted,
  And made a great squealing,
To tell mother bruin
  The fright she was feeling;
So Hoto turned back
  With his load that was yowling,
And heavy, and scratchy,
  And biting and howling;

Till came a great roar,
  And a tramping of bushes,
And the breaking of boughs
  When a mother bear rushes.
He gave a quick glance
  Over one burdened shoulder,
And dropped the young cub
  On a very sharp boulder;

And darted away
  Without parley or blunder,
As roars pierced his ears
  Like the pealing of thunder.
Old bruin was coming;
  He heard her plump-plumping,
And his heart beat a jiggity
  Thumpy-thump thumping!

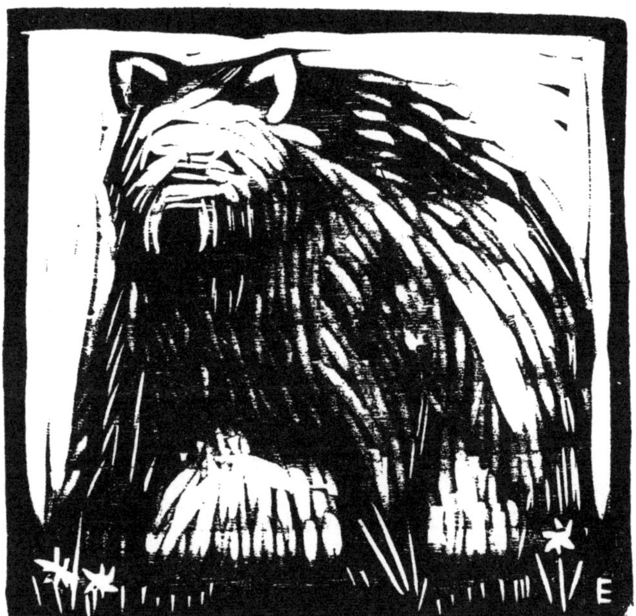

Now nearer and nearer!
  She galloped through shambles!
And Hoto was scratched
  By the thorns of the brambles;
He saw her eyes gleam,
  And he struggled for breath;
She surely would catch him,
  And crush him to death!

He thought of his chances,
  Now better, now waning,
But close on his heels—
  Mercy Me! She was *gaining!*
He almost despaired,
  And his blood was congealing,
When the cub trouble-maker
  Repeated her squealing!

The mother bear paused,
  (While Tee Hoto sped faster)
And turned to her cub
  Which had suffered disaster.
The boy stumbled on
  Till he came to the clearing,
And saw the good caves,
  And forgot all his fearing.

The river stretched out,
  Like a riband of silk,
And he longed for some berries
  And cocoa-nut milk!

GATHERING WOOD

Hunting for wood! Hunting for wood!
Dodo and Toto, as cave children should;
  Busy as bees, and as chirp as a cricket,
  Found a big nest in the midst of a thicket;
Four speckled eggs, and they tasted so nice,
They stopped while they sucked them, as silent as mice.

Hunting for wood! Hunting for wood!
They tried to remember as well as they could;
  Saw a black snake gliding into the bushes,
  Found a big stick and with thrustings and pushes,
Caught him, and killed him, and pulled him in two,
And sat down to eat him, as savages do.

Hunting for wood! Hunting for wood!
It had to be gathered, they well understood.
  Look at the cherry trees, groaning with cherries!
  Crabapples too! And the berries! The berries!
Picked and they picked them; they tasted so sweet,
They had to squat down in the forest to eat.

Food for the Fire! Food for the Fire!
Stack up the branches—Oh! Higher and higher!
  Busy as ants, but the crabapples tumbling,
  Had to be gathered though cave folks were grumbling;
Thick as a carpet, and juicy, and red;
Duty's forgotten while children are fed.

Gathering wood! Gathering wood!
Have to be busy, and thoughtful, and good.
  Snails and large larvae of beetles, and HONEY!
  O for the morn again, golden and sunny!
O what a bundle the darkness to rout!
Gracious! My goodness! The fire is OUT!

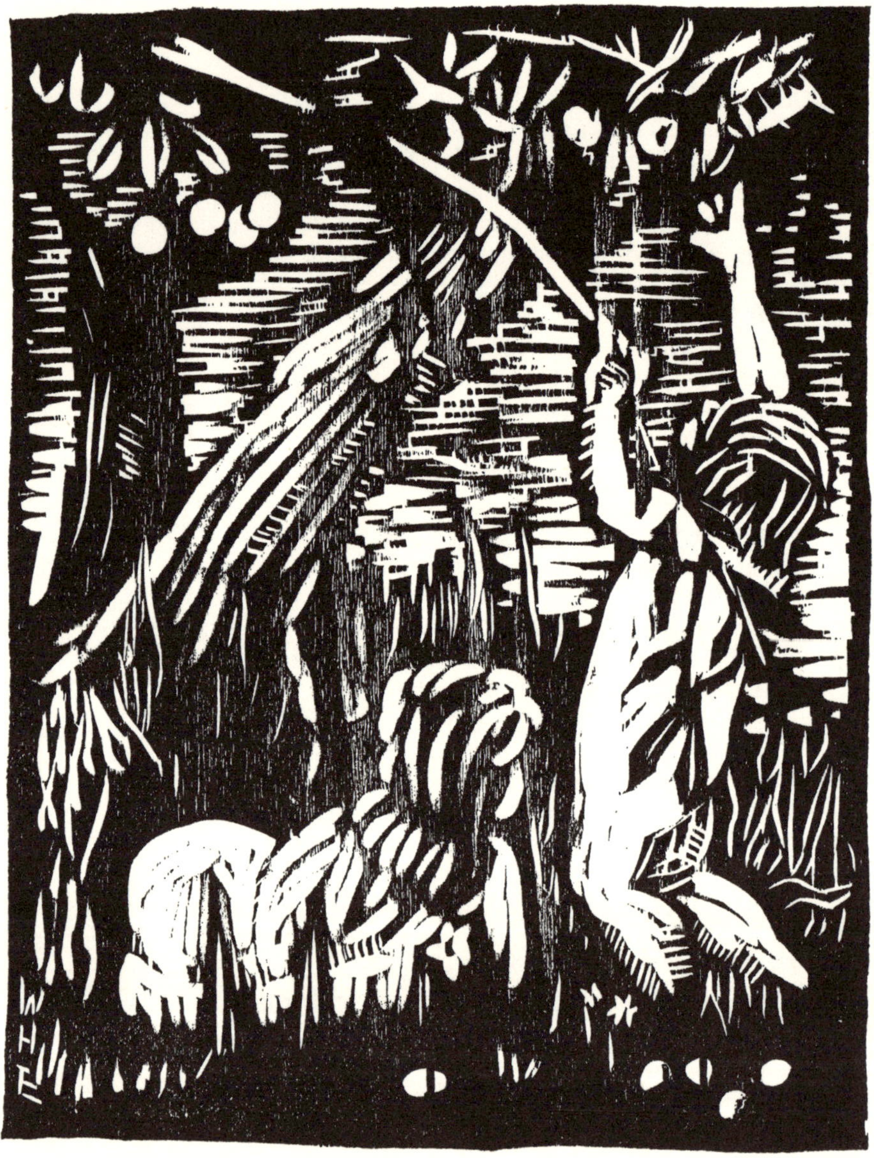

CRABAPPLES TOO

Fire is dead! Fire is dead!
Dodo and Toto, each hanging his head;
  Crawl in the cave where they shiver and cower,
  'Fraid that a tiger may come to devour;
Sorry they didn't remember the wood,
For the blaze of the fire means safety and good!

O for a fire; O for a fire!
Cave people know what it is to desire!
  Now need to hide when the darkness is falling;
  Hungry things creep, and the shadows are crawling;
Every one knows why the Fire is dead,
Dodo and Toto each hanging his head!

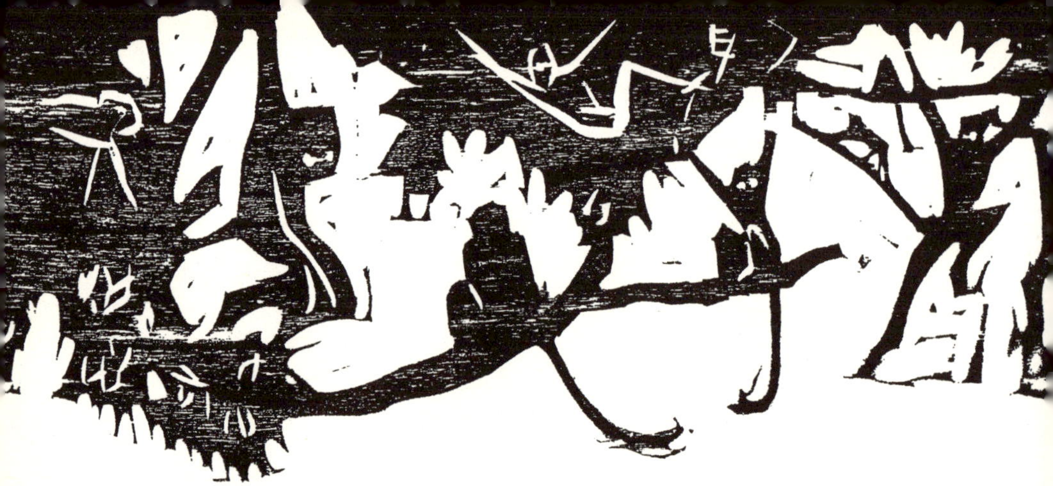

THE TREE PEOPLE

They swung themselves from tree to tree,
By grasping for a limb,
And flung themselves
From very dizzy heights,
And raced aloft among the boughs,
With every passing whim;
And perched on high,
Perceived the jungle sights.

They didn't have a language then;
There wasn't much to say;
They chattered all,
In funny little cries,
To tell of food, or fear, or love,
Or scold their foes away,
Or warn a reckless youth
Against surprise.

They robbed the nests and ate the birds,
Descended too to fish,
And sometimes caught
A juicy little pig;
And everything was eaten raw,
And never saw a dish;
For manners—Oh!
They did not care a fig!

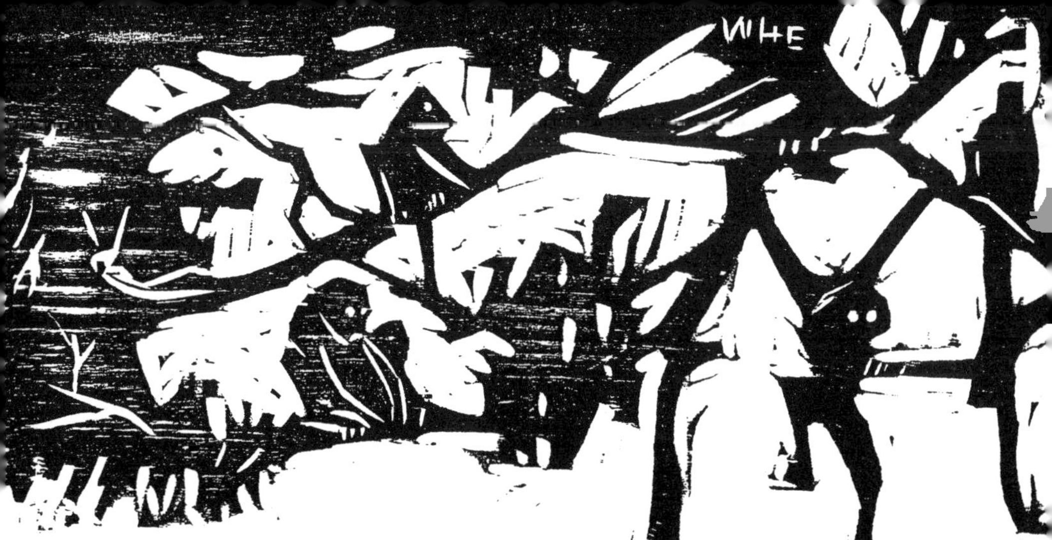

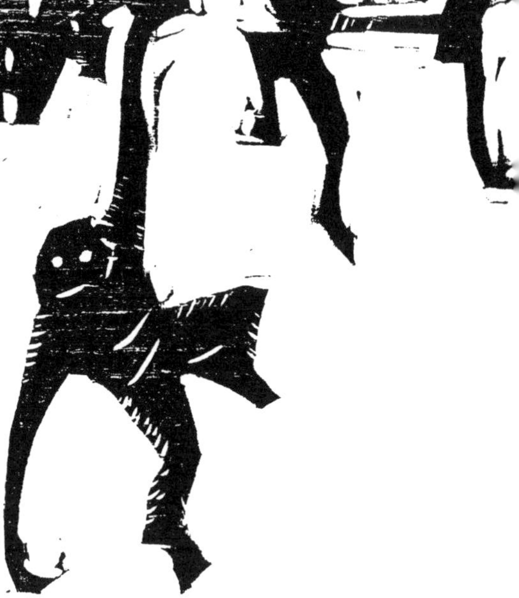

When one was captured by a foe,
The rest all turned to flee,
Though mutual aid
Helps creatures to survive;
Each tree-man had to fight alone,
Was selfish as could be;
It's a wonder any one
Was left alive!

The cave folks all were social,
And acquired tools and speech;
They always helped
A comrade in distress;
And they grew strong because the tribe
Would always fight for each;
Were rather decent
Savages, I guess.

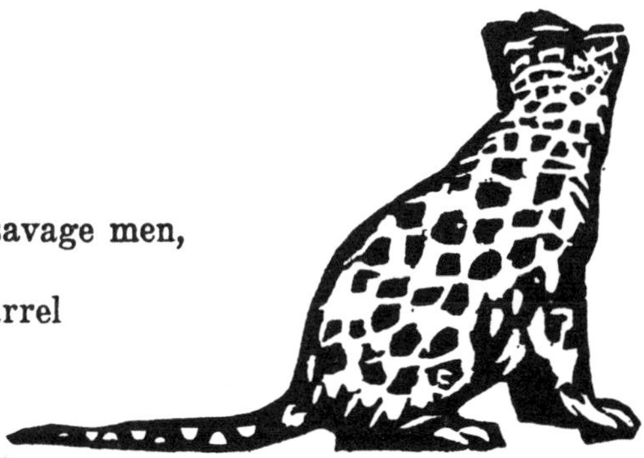

The tigers grew afraid,
And hesitated to attack,
Although it wasn't hard
To slaughter one;
They learned when hunting savage men,
They had to fight the pack,
And they often wished a quarrel
Had not begun.

THE FIRST PRIEST

The chief of the Cave Folks,
  Was tall Strong Arm,
The first on the trail,
  Or to give an alarm;
The longest, the strongest,
  He taught them to know
The paths which were safe,
  And the ways they should go.

But now he was crushed
  By a pain-maddened bear,
Protecting her cubs
  Hid away in her lair.
They buried him deep,
  And they covered his bed,
With earth and with stones
  And they placed at his head,
Pink tubers, and fishes,
  And baskets of meat,
That he might not lack food
  When his spirit would eat.

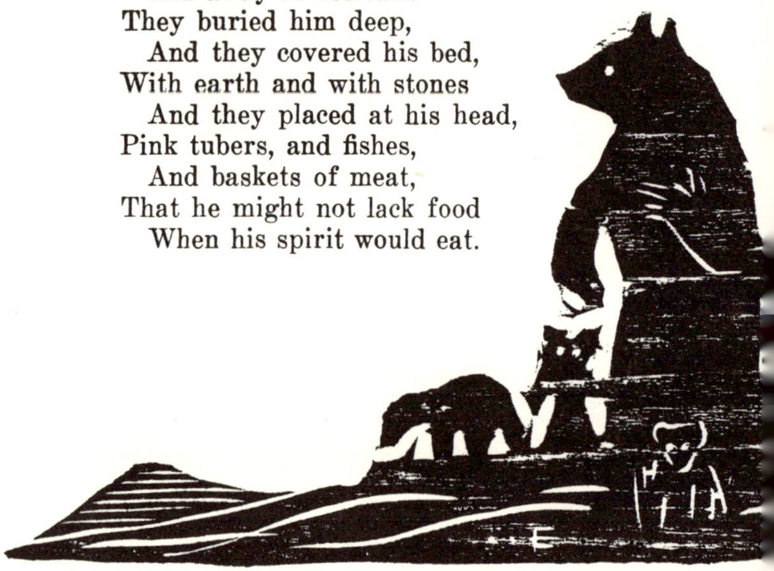

They knew that his spirit
  Was hovering near,
And they made a lament
  To his mythical ear:
"Oh! Spirit", they cried,
  "Pray you tell us the way
"To find a new chief,
  "Lest we wander astray."

And as the nights passed,
  And the people awoke,
The Lazy One
  Fooled all these credulous folk.
"The spirit of Strong Arm
  "Remembers our plight,
"And brings me commands,
  "As I sleep in the night;
"He bids you choose Oof
  "As your chief and your guide,
"And commands me give counsel,
  "For Him, at his side."

And the Cave Folks believed
  In this primitive priest,
And gave him the tenderest meat,
  At the feast.

HOW THE CAVE FOLKS ACQUIRED THE BOW AND ARROW

A stranger came down from the heights one day;
He carried his arrow and bow,
And a cave boy saw wonderful sights at play
As he watched him a-hunting below the bay,
Where the ferns and the gooseberries grow.
He watched from a tree when a boar came by;
The stranger was brave, and the reason why
Was his arrow that sped like a summer sigh—
To slaughter his boar-ship, you know.

And down sat the stranger to eat that day;
His weapon was thrown on the ground,
And heard not the creeping of feet; it lay
In reach when the boy with a bound, the way
A cave boy leaps forth without sound,
He snatched up the bow and the arrows too,
And fled to the woods where the mists were blue,
And back to the horde for he knew he knew
The marvelous prize he had found!

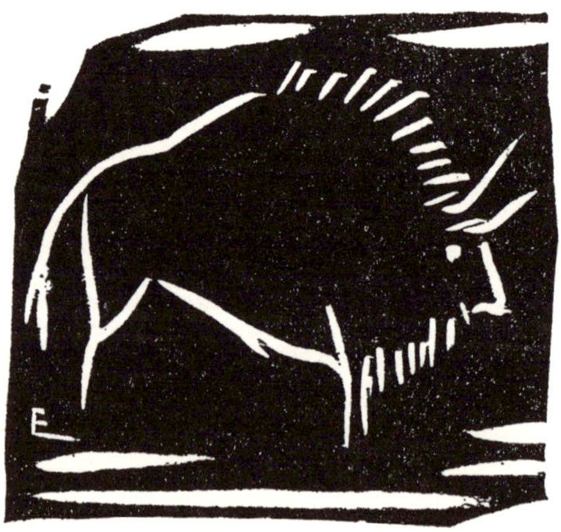

The cave folks made arrows and bow at last,
And carried them early and late;
They hid in the brush when the doe ran past,
And learned to aim surely and straight so fast,
They all took a menacing gait!
They ventured afar where the calves were led,
And elephants trained them, and youngsters fed;
With far-reaching weapons, when all is said,
Enjoyed a most comforting state!

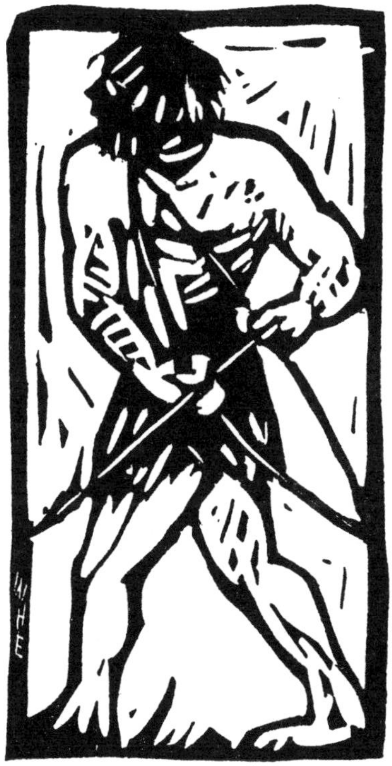

HUNTING

A deer sped down a gentle slope,
  To join the grazing herd;
She leaped before the rowdy wind,
  As lightly as a bird.

Her nostrils twitched to catch the scent
  Of wolves upon the trail;
Her sharp ears cocked to left and right,
  For sounds borne on the gale.

Before her, in a wide ravine,
  O-pot-o-wallo hid,
And waited, patient as the hills,
  Concealing gorse amid.

Long had he stalked a foolish shoat,
  Which straggled far behind,
Until it caught the hunter's scent,
  In the revealing wind,

And summoned all the other pigs,
  With squeals of shrill alarm,
And scampered to the steaming swamp,
  Where it was safe from harm.

O-pot-o-owallo thought about
  The hungry tribe, and then
Crept up among the hillocks,
  Patiently to hunt again.

His cunning was rewarded for
  A message from his ear,
Announced the sound of hoof-beats,
  And the coming of a deer.

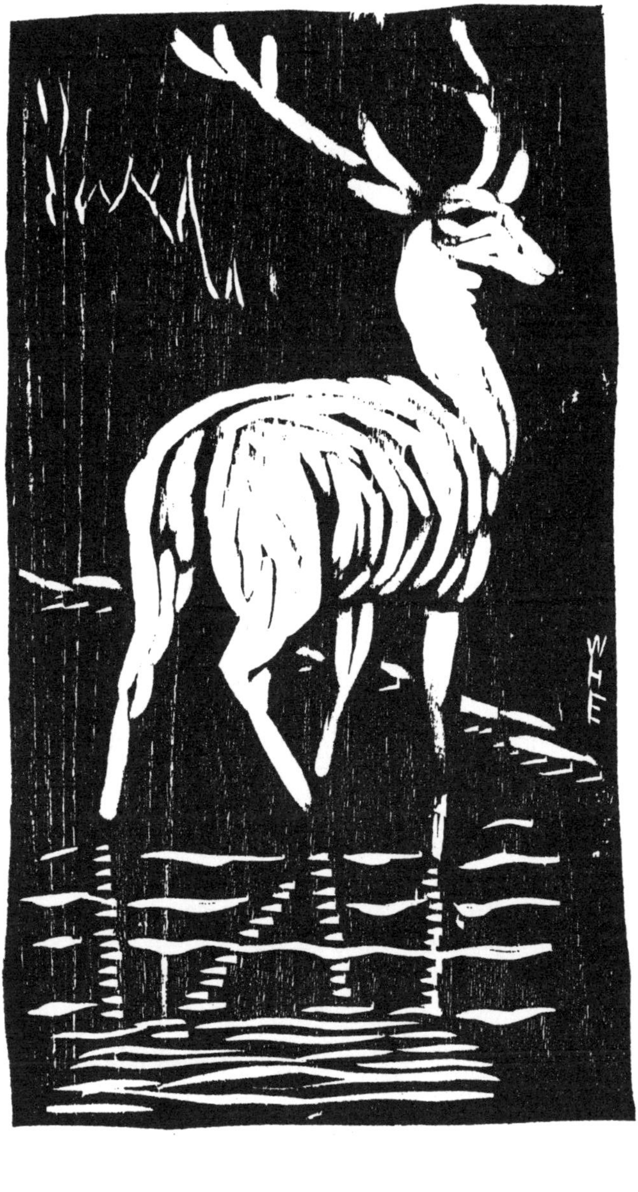

He saw her cross a shallow stream,
  And climb its mossy bank;
He watched her at the salt-lick,
  Where the herbs were green and rank;

Her coat was soft and shining,
  Of an autumn brown and red;
And O-pot-o-wallo saw
  A snowy star upon her head.

And nearer now; still on and on,
  He heard the welcome sound,
And saw her leap a scraggy crag,
  With one exultant bound.

O-pot-o-wallo raised his bow,
  And thought of all the braves,
Of the women and the children,
  And the hunger in the caves.

The hunter aimed; his arrow flew,
  Straight to the star of white;
And O-pot-o-wallo gloried: "Oh!
  "The tribe shall eat tonight!"

BURIED POTATOES

Little Big Nose did not know,
How the wild potatoes grow;
  But he buried four one day;
  Then forgot and ran away.

Warm the summer sun shone down,
On the earth all rich and brown;
  Berries blue and berries red
  Lifted each a ripened head,

And when August showers fell,
Drank and nodded: "All is well."
  Cave folks need to hunt for meat,
  Which is sometimes all they eat;

Not a man among them knew,
How the juicy tubers grew.
  Little Big Nose dug one day,
  Where his four potatoes lay;

There he found a wondrous prize;
Called the folks with dancing eyes.
  Not the four potatoes, he
  Found, but nearly thirty-three!

Cave folks did not understand,
How the farmers use the land,
  But they wanted to decide,
  How potatoes multiplied.

Came a wise and ancient man,
Squatted as a savage can;
  Told them how the thing was done:
  Little tubers, one by one,

Were by big potatoes laid,
Buried deep and unafraid.
  So they covered fish and meat,
  Hoping to grow more to eat;

But they found no fishes there;
Found no deer chops any where,
  Though the wild potatoes grew,
  Little tubers, pink and new!

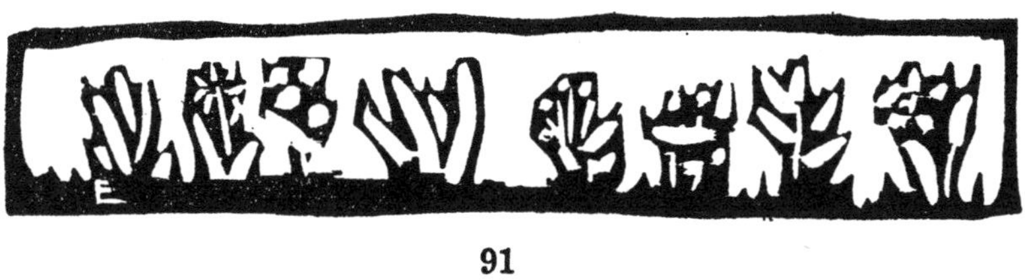

THE NANNY GOAT

The Brave One saw a nanny goat,
  While hunting in the hills;
    The nanny had a little kid,
    Which tried the things her mother did,
  And leaped the rocks and rills.

And so she tumbled down a gorge;
  Her plight was very grave,
    The tumble crushed her clumsy feet,
    The hunter heard her piteous bleat,
  And bore her to his cave.

The hunter took her to his cave,
  Below the rocky steep;
    He wondered how she could be fed,
    And made for her a mossy bed,
  And soon she fell asleep.

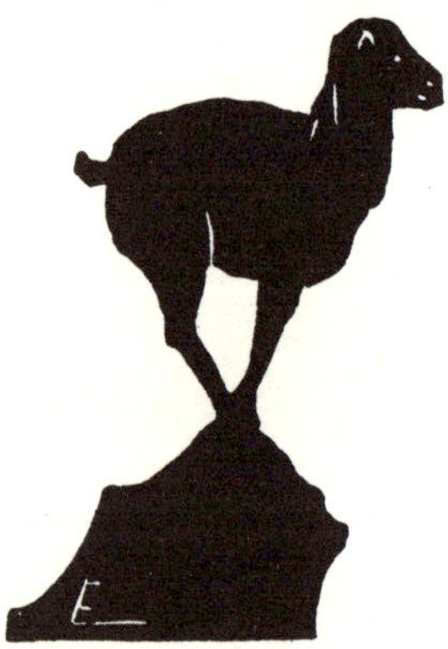

But when the morning sun arose,
  As every day it did,
    The nanny goat had come to dwell,
    And liked her ample quarters well;
  Had come to nurse her kid.

The hunter fed her tender grass,
  And often let her range;
    He learned to milk her every day,
    And here her kid could safely play;
  It was a fair exchange.

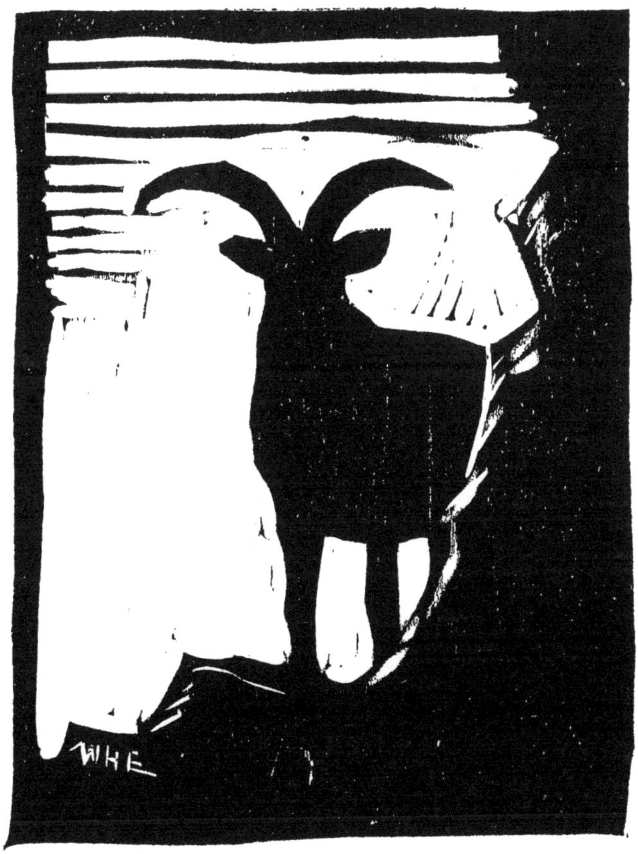

WOOING

Cock-Ear met a lion;
He looked her in the eye,
And snapped his fingers in her face,
As he was going by.

If he had had his arrows—
The things he might have done!
He said the menace in his eyes
Had set her on the run.

Cock-Ear told The Sparrow,
His tale of bravery.
She said the only thing it lacked
Was authenticity!

Big Tooth wooed the maidens,
In quite another way.
While hunting in a deep ravine
He found a bed of clay.

White clay! Red clay!
Purple and brown and chrome!
He painted his body from brow to heels,
And dazzled the folks at home.

Clay dyes! Red eyes!
Purple and gold his breast,
With stripes on his legs like our Easter eggs,
No wonder he swelled his chest!

New styles! Clay wiles!
The maids gathered round to see
The beautiful spots! The streaks and the dots!
By the hand of an artist, free.

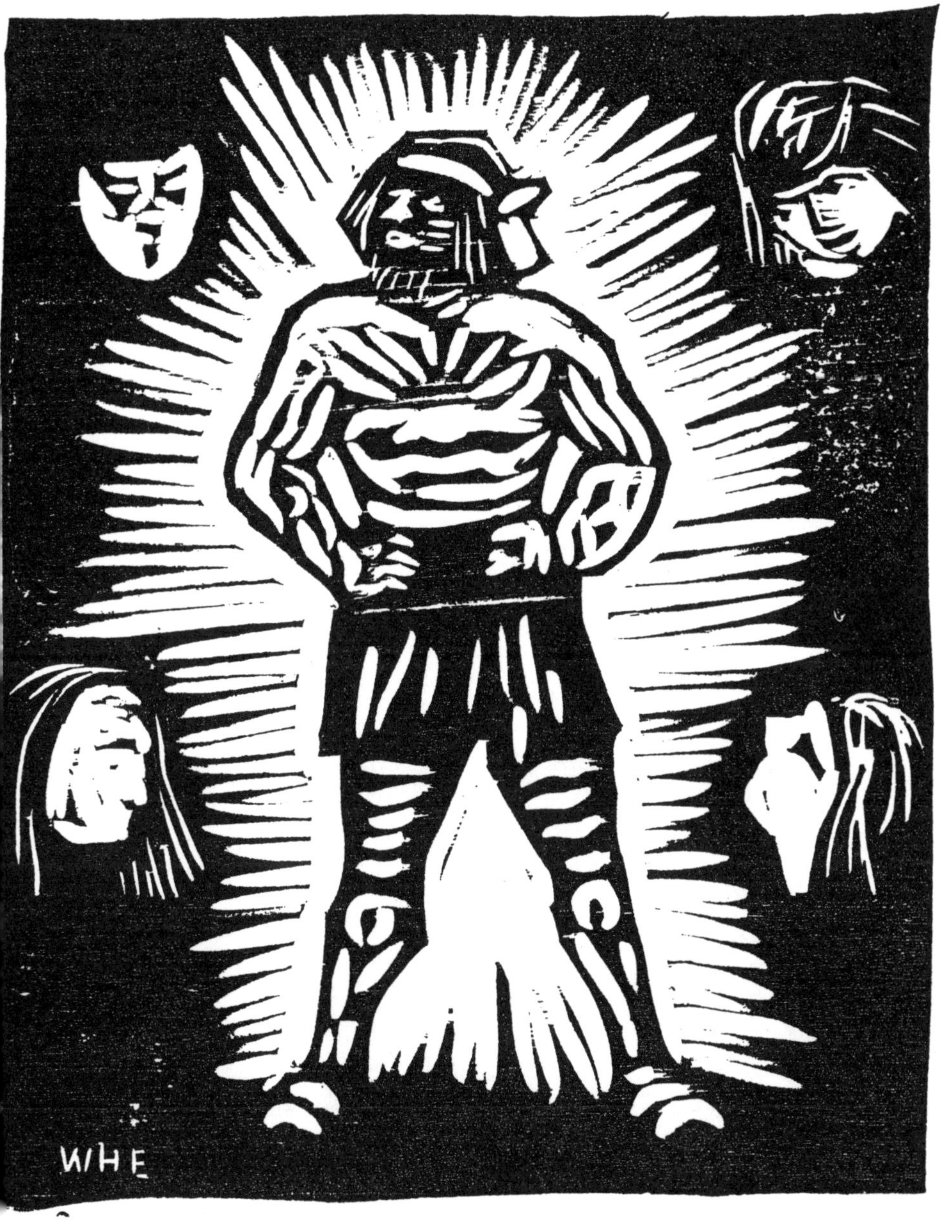
WHE

THE ELEPHANT SAID

The elephant said: "I'm not afraid,
"I'm not afraid; I'm not afraid!
"I own the forests, pools and glade,
  "I wander where I will.
    "The other beasts all run away,
    "All run away; all run away;
    "They never stop to say 'Good day',
  "And I may eat my fill."

The tiger said: "My fangs are long,
"My fangs are long; my fangs are long!
"My claws are very sharp and strong,
  "And I shall always reign.
    "The herds of deer are only mine,
    "Are only mine; are only mine;
    "The cubs and whelps and calves and swine,
  "For this is my domain."

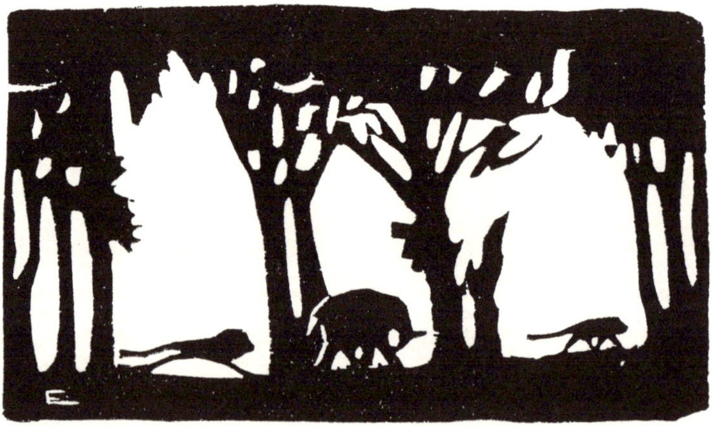

The lion said: "I am the King,
"I am the King; I am the King!
"I'll never run from any thing,
  "That learns to climb or leap.
    "The tiger will not bother me,
    "Not bother me! Not bother me;
    "I'll make him climb a banyan tree,
  "Where all the monkeys sleep."

A cave boy he was very small,
Was very small, was very small;
He could not fight these beasts at all,
  And so he built a fire;
    The elephant fled away in fear,
    The tiger left a stricken deer,
    The lion said: "This menace near
  "Is not of my desire!"

And so the boy was safe at last,
Was safe at last; was safe at last;
He built a fire big and fast,
  The woods were filled with smoke.
    He made a torch as best he could,
    As best he could, as best he could,
    And marched in triumph through the wood,
  To show the tribal folk.

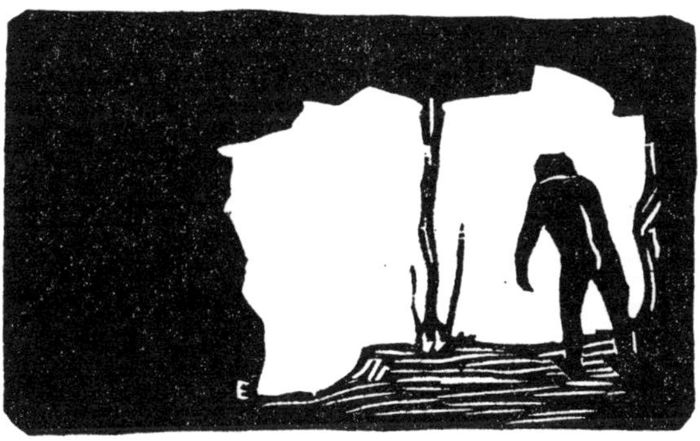

HOW MUM MUM IGNITED A FIRE

Mum Mum squatted on a rock,
To make a knife of flint;
He hacked away with clumsy care;
The chips and flakes flew everywhere,
Of dark and leaden tint.

He hammered on with all his might,
Till sparks began to fly.
He thought: "Perhaps I've found a way,
"To make a fire every day;
"At any rate, I'll try."

He brought the feathers of a bird,
And juicy knots of pine,
And scattered them to left and right,
So they would by a spark ignite;
It was a wise design.

He pounded on a piece of flint,
Till sparks flew all around;
And saw the fire's magic ways;
When feathers flung a tiny blaze,
He danced upon the ground!

He fed the fire boughs and logs,
And fled to tell the horde,
Which hurried forward in the shade,
To see the thing his hands had made,
And Mum Mum's fire roared!

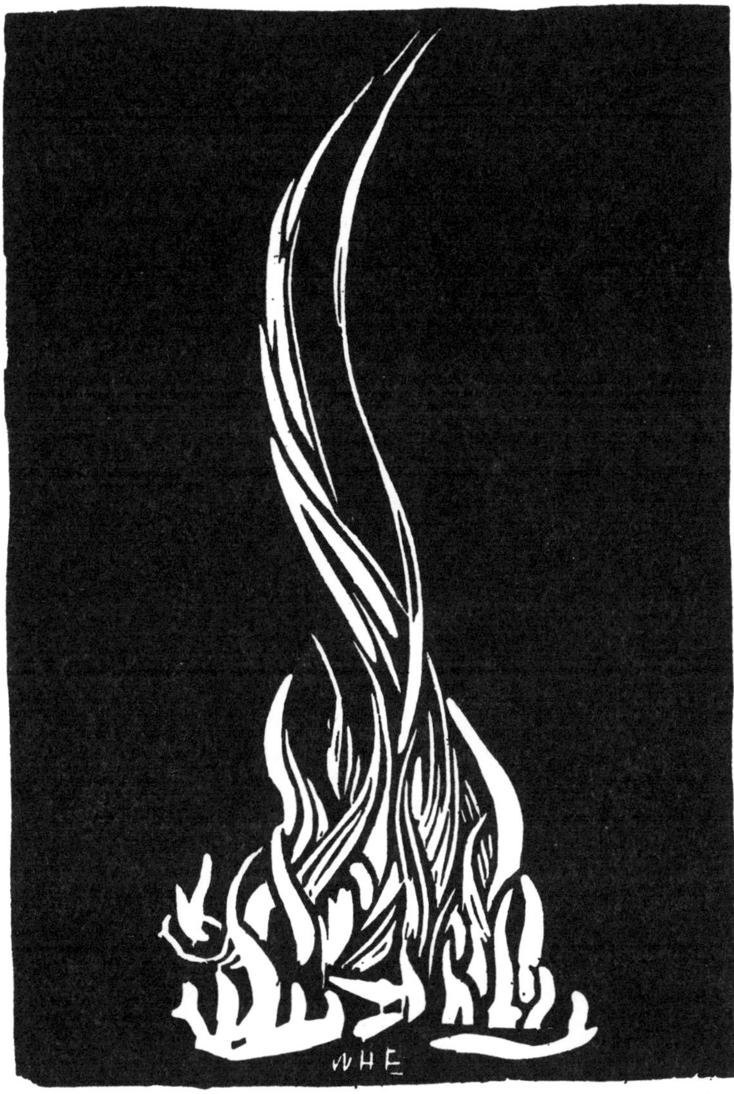
WHE

PUZZLES AND THINGS

He stared at his reflection in the water,
And gathered stones to drive the youth away;
He brandished spear, for he was ripe for slaughter,
But his water image mocked him from the bay;
He couldn't understand it, for the thing was always there,
And when he dived he could not find the fellow any where;
So down he sat upon the bank,
And gave him stare for stare.

And when he walked, this Neolithic youngster,
He saw his shadow pacing with his stride,
And ran a dozen metres to evade him,
But the silent fellow galloped at his side;
He could not understand it, and he racked his feeble mind,
The shadow seemed to run as fast as any startled hind,
And so he glowered at the shade
He could not leave behind.

And when he found a spring among the caverns,
And whooped his joy, an eerie play began;
The walls caught up his song of happy triumph,
And echoes sent it flying back again,
Repeated every song he sung, and mimicked every call;
He could not understand the voices in the cavern wall,
And hunted for a human trail,
Which was not there at all.

And when he fell asleep upon his bear skin,
He often dreamed and thought his dreams were true;
He killed a giant mammoth with his arrow,
And forests full of hairy people slew;

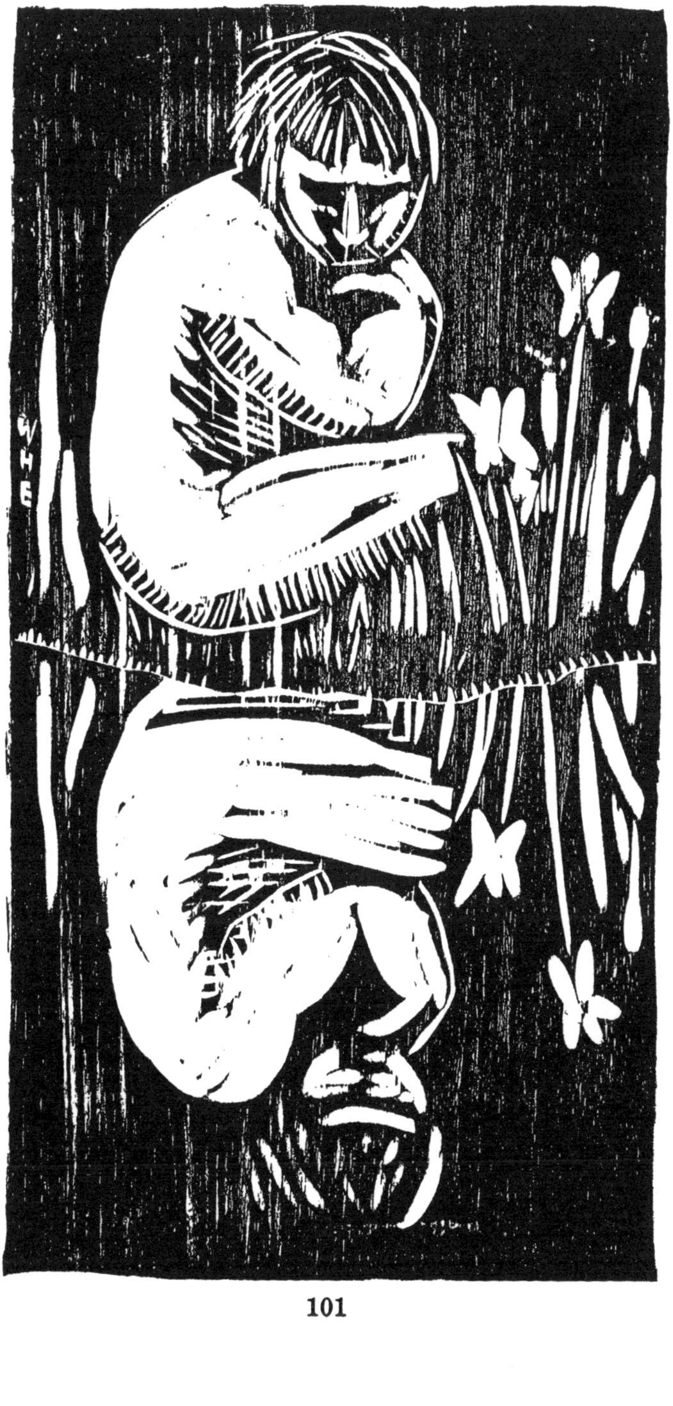
WHE

But when he waked and bragged about his valor, strong
and deep,
The folks who tend the fire, and the silent watches keep,
Shook their heads in grave denial:
"You were in the cave asleep!"

He sometimes saw the dead chief in his dreaming,
And heard his voice commanding all the men;
He thought the dead were only dead in seeming,
And fall asleep to one day hunt again;
He gazed at his reflection, and his shadow, and he thought:
The world is filled with spirit folks, and puzzles spirit-
wrought;
It is wisdom to respect them, and
I had as lief as not.

THE CAMEL

The camel is a desert brute
  With thickly padded feet
Which travel through the burning sands,
  And do not feel the heat.

Her humps are full of food, you know,
  So when there is no grazing,
She sucks it up and has a meal,
  When desert sun is blazing;

A dozen pails of water drinks
  To last her on her ways,
Four stomachs full and these, we learn,
  Refresh her many days.

She carries food and water tanks,
  (Beneath her silken hide)
And burdens, too, of goods to sell,
  And merchants who must ride.

And when she dies her owner finds
  Her hair is soft and sweet
For making brushes, shawls, and, too,
  Her flesh is good to eat.

A very, very useful beast
  The camel is to man,
She bears him over burning wastes
  Which nothing else may span.

THE TADPOLE

The pollywogs,
  When they leave the eggs,
Are born without feet,
  And they have no legs;
Are born without legs,
  So they cannot jump,
As their mothers do over
  A log or stump.

They live in the water,
  And there they stay,
To hunt for their food,
  And to grow and play.
The tadpoles are fishes,
  With fins and tails,
And breathe through their gills,
  Though they have no scales.

They wiggle and swim,
  And they dart about,
And they grow, and they grow,
  Till their legs come out,
When they lose their fins,
  And they learn to leap,
And croak in the swamps,
  When we're half asleep.

They hide like a leaf,
  In the tangled grass,
And leap to the streams,
  When the black snakes pass.
Oh! Isn't it wonderful
  Down in the bogs,
Where the tadpoles grow up
  Into beautiful frogs!

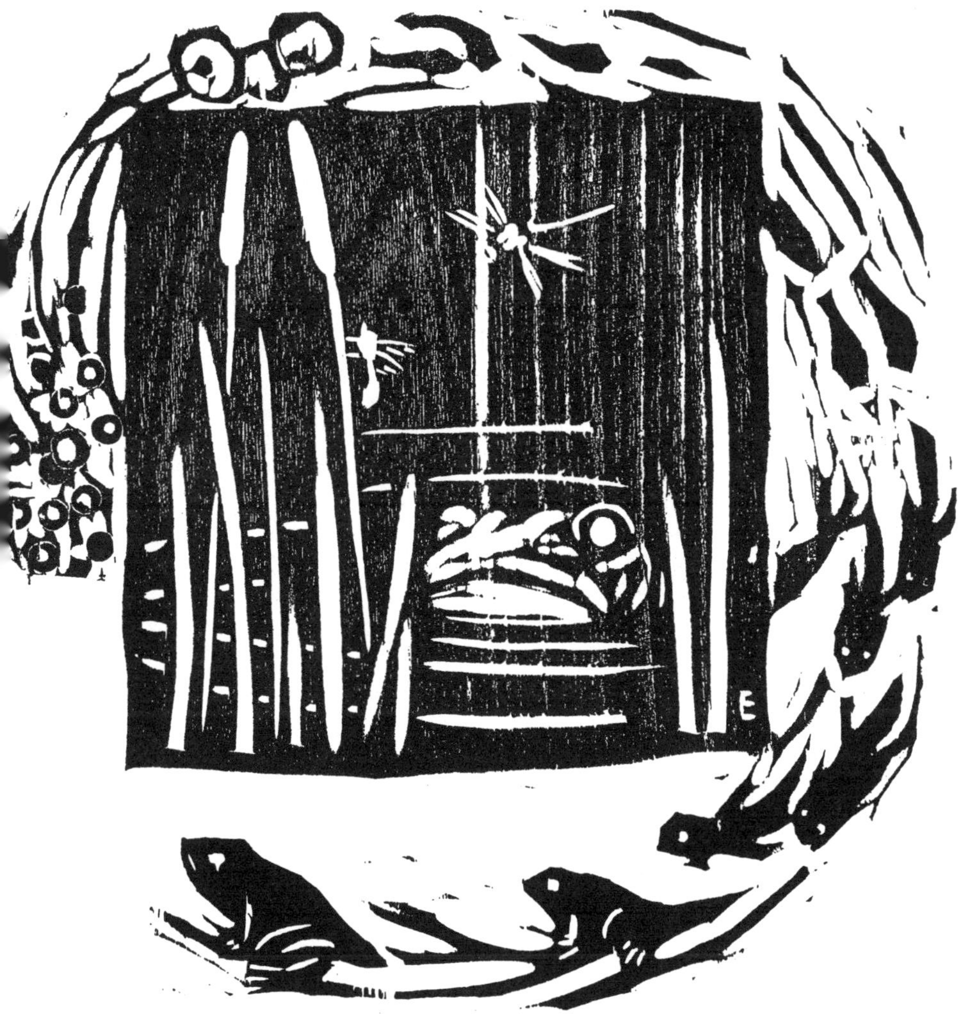

ON THE BOTTOM OF THE OCEAN

If we could make a diving bell,
  Or build a submarine,
And journey far below the waves,
  Through miles of blue and green,
We'd find a wonder-world upon
  The bottom of the ocean,
Of water sprites, with scarlet lights,
  And fishes in commotion.

We'd stand upon the ocean bed,
  Down underneath the steamers,
And watch the lilies of the sea
  Wave high their airy streamers.
We'd wear an iron diving suit,
  That strange fish might not flout us,
And linger in the water woods,
  To watch the folks about us.

Where dainty little nether trees,
  With purple lights a-glimmer,
Like fairy apples on the boughs,
  Are making shadows shimmer;
See glossy sponge of filagree,
  As fragile as the foaming
Of eager breakers on the shore,
  When they return from roaming.

And see the corals building high,
  As tall as rocky mountain,
Their shining lights invading dark,
  Like diamonds in a fountain;
They flash their magic, elfin lamps,
  Like lanterns in a village,
And turn them off when we approach,
  Lest we have come for pillage.

The little fish are swimming past,
  Their lamps of blue are lighted,
But when they see a larger fish,
  They turn them off, affrighted.
Here steals a monster in the dark,
  His mouth is wide and yawning,
But little fishes' lights are dimmed;
  They saw the danger dawning.

The monster lights his emerald torch,
  That grows his nose a-striding,
And searches in the water-wood,
  For little fish in hiding.
They watch among the coral trees,
  And see the hungry stranger
Glide past and upward on his way,
  And they are free from danger.

The star fish on the bottom lie,
  Like candles incandescent;
Their shining arms are emerald green,
  And glowing phosphorescent;
The water meadows are in bloom,
  In deep and hidden bowers,
And flaunt their purple, red and gold,
  And blue and yellow flowers.

The lilies of the sea are here,
  With roots that hold them tightly,
A link between the plant and beast,
  If teachers tell us rightly;
The yellow sea anemone,
  A sea cow with her baby,
Which nurses like a barnyard calf,
  And quite as clumsy, maybe.

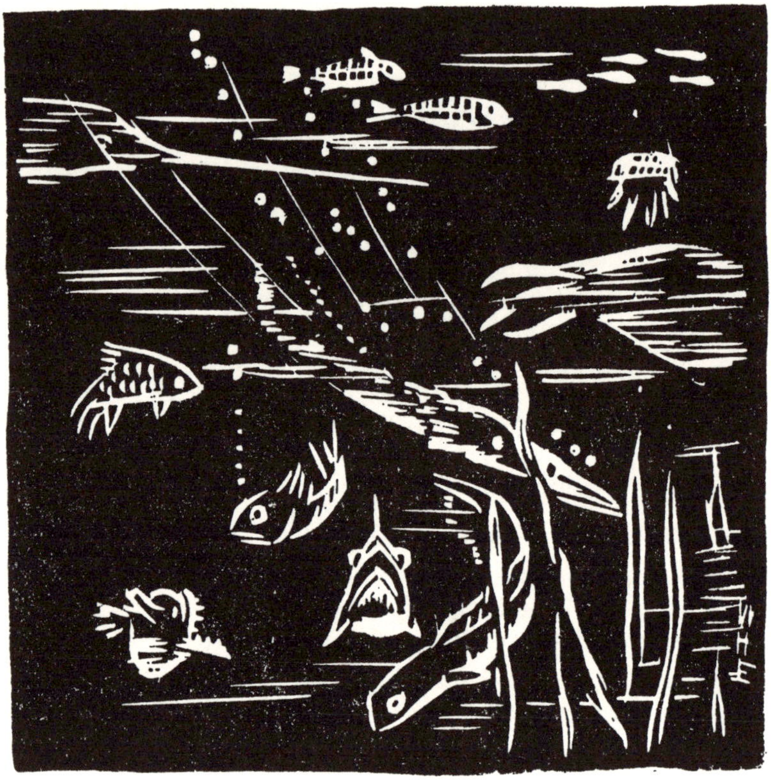

The flower-beasties have balloons,
  To take their families riding,
And rise above the water trees,
  To learn the sun is hiding.
O what a wonder-world it is,
  Way down amid the ocean!
With ruby snails and giant whales,
  And fishes in commotion!

THE GOAT

Goats eat papers;
  Goats like bags,
And worn-out shoes for their desserts,
  And goats love rags.

Goats eat baskets;
  And goats eat string,
And toy balloons, and wooden spoons,
  And almost any thing.

Their fathers lived on hilltops,
  As high as they could climb,
Because the savage wolves below
  Were hunting all the time.

The hills were bare and craggy,
  There wasn't any grass;
They had to eat the fibrous weeds,
  That grew along the pass.

The weeds were tough as leather,
  And dry as saw-dust too;
Their stomachs labored to digest
  These shrubs the goats would chew.

And so their sons and daughters,
  The goats we have to-day,
Can live on hose and worn-out clothes
  That folks have thrown away.

Goats eat papers;
  Goats like bags,
And worn-out clothes for their dessert,
  And goats love rags!

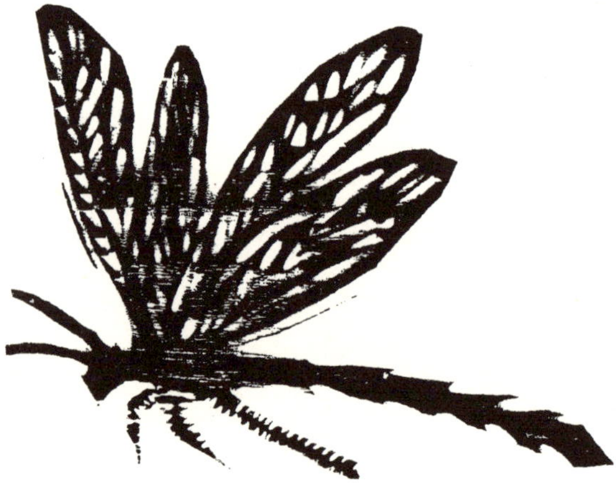

THE ANT LION

They call her "Oolie oolie bug";
  She builds a deadly snare
For ants and fleas and crippled bees
  To walk in unaware.

A funnel of the sand she makes,
  And down below its end,
She hides beneath the sand to wait
  For bugs the Fates may send.

They wander in; they tumble down;
  Try to escape the trap,
While sand rolls down beneath their feet,
  And "oolie" feigns a nap.

They struggle, frantic, for the top;
  They nearly reach it when
The "oolie" throws sand over them—
  And down they roll again.

She grabs them with her mandibles,
  And clips their legs in two,
And drags them underneath the sand,
  To bite and suck and chew,

Until at last the "oolie" grows
  Soft gauzy wings to fly,
And finds a mate and seeks a nest
  For "oolies" by and by.

She kills a worm, and digs a hole,
  And drags him down below,
And lays her eggs upon the grub
  For "oolies" when they grow.

Then off she flies for tiny stones,
  To block the cosy nest,
And hides it all 'neath grains of sand,
  And swings away to rest.

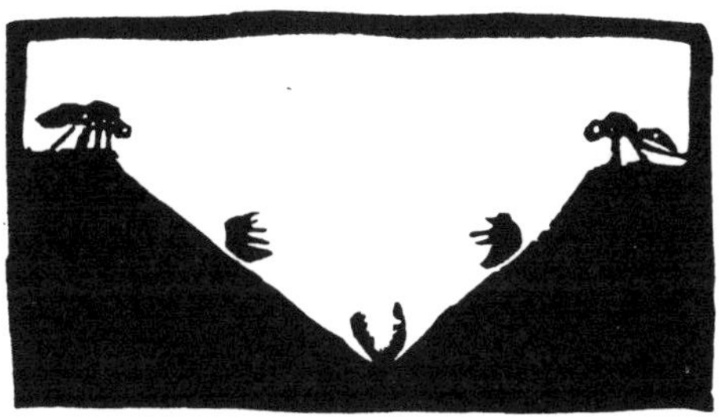

IF EVERY THING GREW UP

If every little cherry stone
  Became a cherry tree,
And every egg the fishes laid
  Grew up to swim to sea,
    The world would be a funny place;
    I fear it could not find the space,
    For you and me and cousin Grace
  To live contentedly.

The cherry trees would fill the streets,
  And where the houses band,
And farms and woods. The cherry trees
  Would cover all the land!
    The sea would be a seething mass
    Of fish where steaming vessels pass,
    And you and I—Alack! Alas!
  Would have no place to stand!

The more I think, the more I know,
  I hate to see things die;
And though I cannot eat enough
  Of mother's cherry pie,
    Perhaps we'd better not complain,
    While things in status quo remain,
    But take the joys that we may gain,
  As every day runs by.

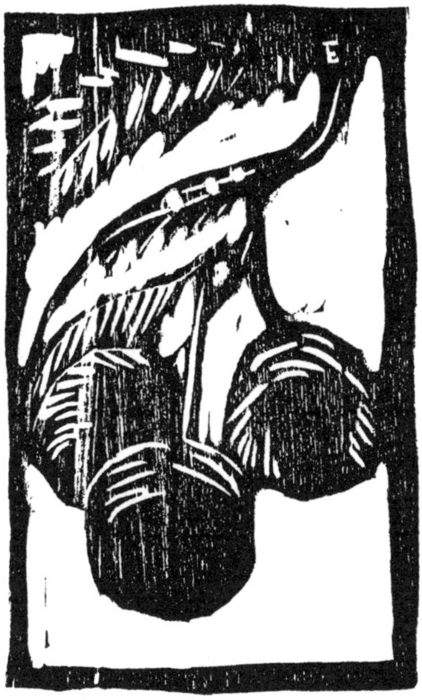

WHERE DOES ALL THE WATER GO?

Where does it go when the water dries,
In the bubbling brook where we make mud pies?

When the days grow warm and the sun shines hot,
And the water dries in the flower pot?

Where does it go when the water man
Drives by with his great big sprinkling can?

He whistles and laughs at the lazy drones,
And flushes and splashes the paving stones;

But the sun shines down, while he seems to say:
"The water may fall, but it will not stay."

And he's surely right for the clock ticks on,
And in less than a hour, the wet's all gone!

What makes it vanish, the water and steam,
When the kettle boils like a geyser's stream?

When the pot burns dry, and it spoils the stew?
I know all about it; do you? And you?

It swells and expands till it grows so light,
That it journeys aloft in a magic flight,

In a magic flight that we cannot see,
But it promises comfort to you and me.

It rises and rises, and soars on high,
To form all the clouds in the azure sky;

Till the wind blows cold, and it turns to rain,
And falls to the earth to refresh the grain,

And gladden the fields as the farmers know,
Who plow up the fields and who reap and sow

The wheat that makes flour and loaves of bread,
In so many lands, that the world is fed!

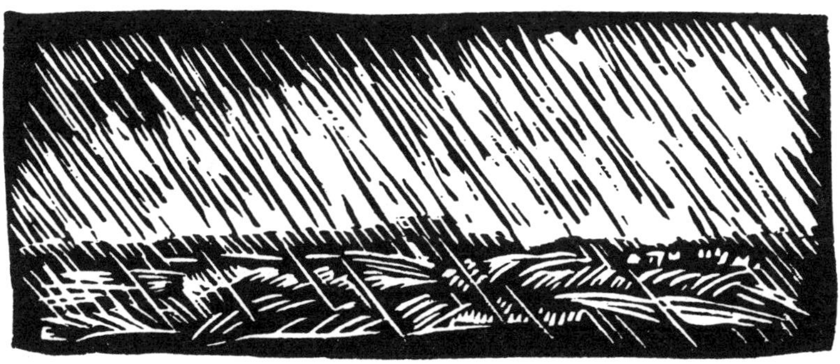

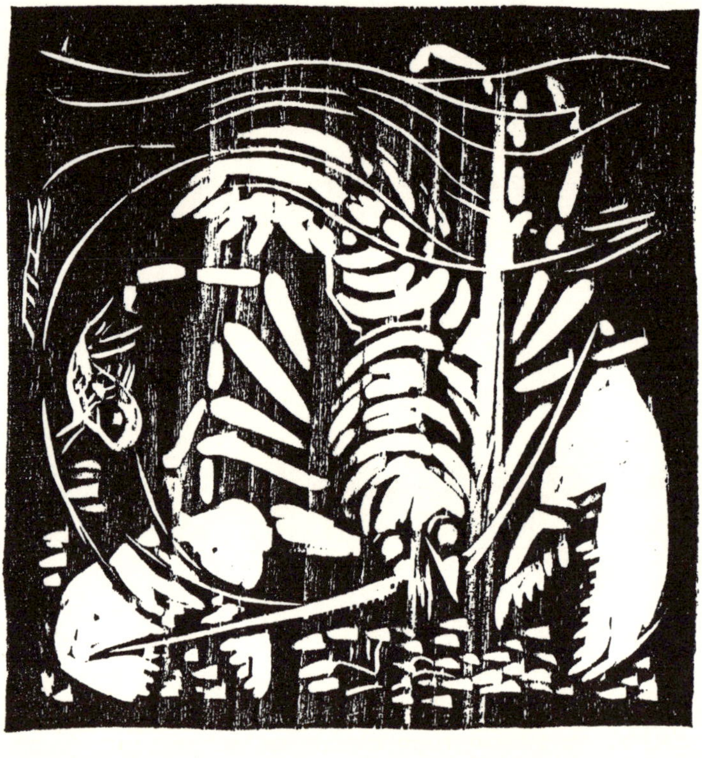

GRAVITATION AND THE LOBSTER

The lobster is a clumsy shrimp,
He ambles like a clown;
To tell when he is right side up,
Or he is upside down,
He never can unless a grain
Of sand is in his ear,
And when it hurts, he knows that he
Is in a posture queer.

He fears he'll never reach his home,
Nor find his water bed,
And knows as well as we that he
Is standing on his head.
He turns and twists himself around,
Until his ear can tell
Him he is walking properly,
And everything is well.

* * *

The lobster is a clumsy shrimp,
He ambles like a clown,
But he is always glad to know,
He isn't upside down!

THE SHEEP JUMPING OVER A FENCE

Way up on the heights
  Where the paths are narrow,
The sheep that could leap
  Like a flying arrow,
Over brooks that dashed,
  From the mountain tops,
Over yawning gaps
  Where a canyon drops,
Escaped from the panther
  Which came to slay,
And brought up their lambkins
  To leap and play.

The leader led them,
  A wise old ram;
He taught all the ewes
  And each frisky lamb;
He led them and bade them
  Obey his call,
Where the cliffs rise sheer,
  Lest they veer and fall.
They could not see
  Where he led them through
Defiles which were hazardous,
  Old, or new.

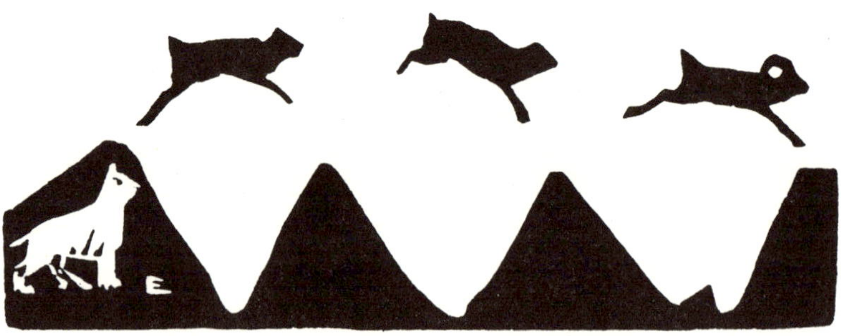

But their footsteps dropped,
  Where his own feet fell;
They sprang with his leapings,
  And all was well;
For one little lurch
  To the West or East,
Might mean that the jackals
  Below would feast!
When they could not see
  What the old ram knew,
They copied precisely
  The things he'd do.

And that's why our sheep,
  When they leap a fence,
Demand not the "whither?"
  And care not "whence?"
But follow the ram,
  Who makes known the way,
And yield to his summons
  The whole long day;
Their grandmothers taught them,
  (Perhaps you've guessed)
That the ways of the ram
  In the lead were best.

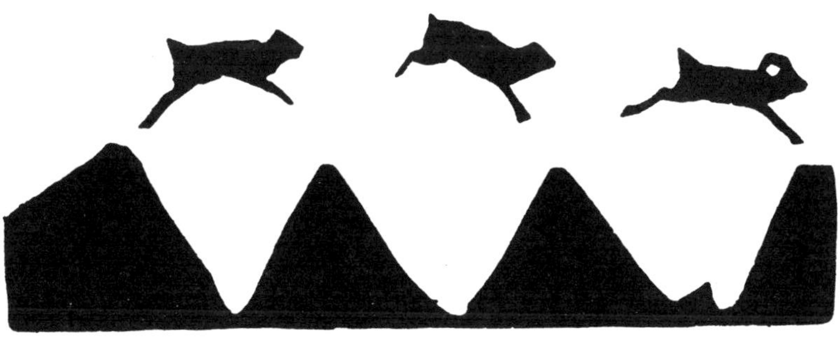

THE MUD TURTLE

If you watch when the mud turtle's
  Feigning a nap,
You will notice he uses
  His mouth for a trap,
And catches big bugs
  With a snippity snap;
And dives in the stream
  With a flap!

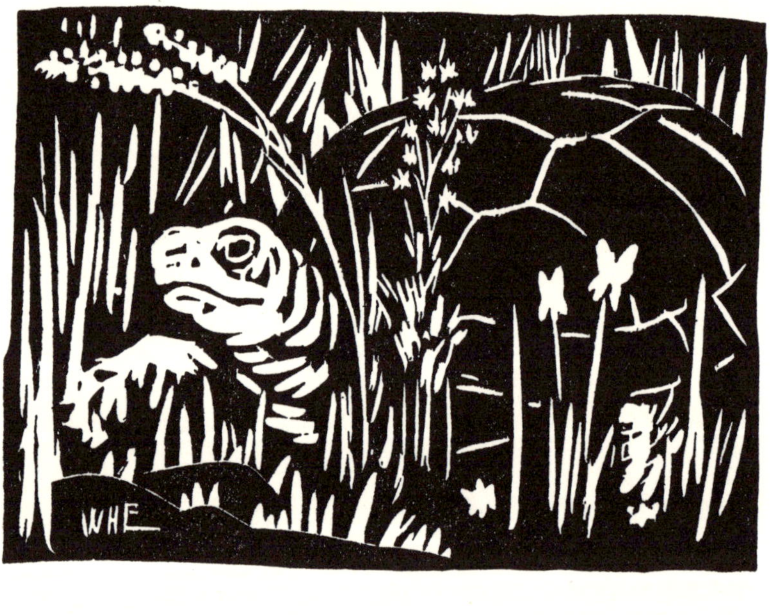

He's without any ribs;
  It is commonly known,
He was born very strangely,
  Without a back-bone,
But he has a great shell,
  Which is hard as a stone,
And he lives in it,
  Wears it—alone.

Yes, the turtle has something
  The larger beasts lack,
He takes it along
  Like a tent in a pack;
He is always at home;
  Shows a wonderful knack—
When he carries his house—
  On his back!

A dog comes along,
  But his head is inside;
His legs are pulled in;
  He continues to hide;
And nothing can harm him;
  He's still as a mouse,
Till it's safe
  To peep out of his house.

THE ATTACK OF THE JUNGLE HORDE

The waters came down from the mountains and hills,
In freshets and streams, like a torrent that spills
  Far over the banks, inundating the wood;
  And they covered the earth where the swamp jungles
      stood.

The jungle hordes rushed in a wild fleeing pack,
Each man for himself, with a club on his back,
  And sought the high lands, where they cautiously crept,
  To slay the cave folks where they peacefully slept.

But the dingo awoke, for she heard them afar,
And she barked to arouse the cave people to war;
  The tribe folks awoke, and so soft were their words,
  They were like the night songs of the twittering birds.

Their hands seized their bows, while their tongues wove a
      plan,
To demolish the foes and to safeguard the clan:
  The women and children remained in the caves,
  With their backs to the wall that a cave savage craves;

While the men took their weapons, and hid in the brush,
To attack when the horde should appear with a rush.
  The cannibals came in the still of the night,
  While the flames from the fire threw a flickering light.

They cautioned in gestures, and signals, and signs,
And revealed their disjointed and cruel designs,
  When the chief of the cave people shouted a word,
  And the leaves in the bushes were instantly stirred,

And their arrows leaped forth from the depths of the
wood,
And the jungle folks huddled or fell where they stood;
For little of speech had this cannibal band;
They gestured, and grunted, made signs with a hand.

In fleeing they fell on each other and fought,
For they never could tell who the man they had caught.
(It is fatal to talk in a primitive war
With gestures at night to show just who you are.)

Their hands were so busy with clubbing and fight,
It were madness to try to set any one right;
But the cave men called out so their comrades might
know,
Where a friend was engaged with a blood-thirsty foe.

So gone were the foes by the breaking of day;
They were dead; they were wounded, or driven away.
And thus when the savage acquired a speech,
And shared with each other, and struggled for each,

And learned to shoot far with his arrow and bow,
And cared for his children and helped them to grow,
He drove all before him and conquered the earth,
When his hands were set free to bring new things to
birth.

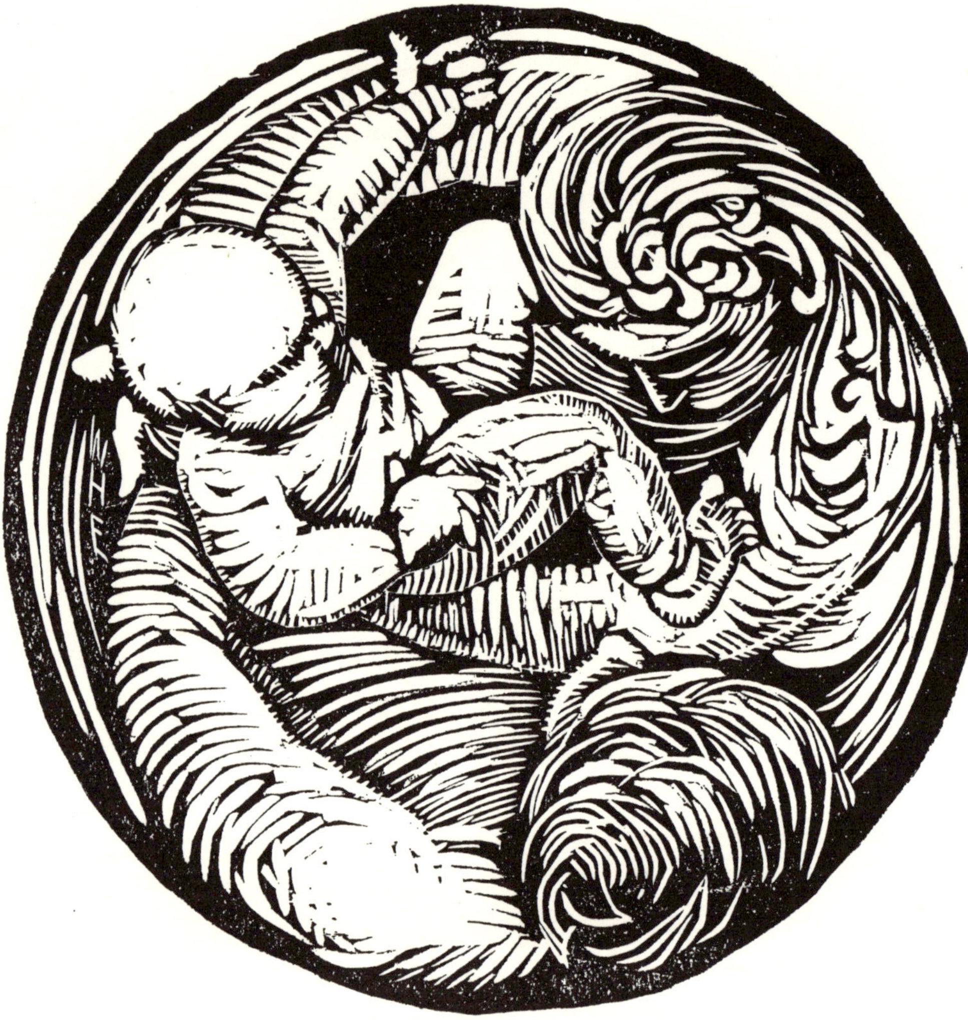